Vodka Classified

Contents

INTRODUCTION

Vodka, in case you hadn't noticed, is everywhere. It has for several years now been the major growth product in the international spirits market. Each year it puts on another few percentage points and, in certain parts of the world, its increase is little short of phenomenal. Between 2002 and 2006, sales in the Asia-Pacific region rose by 22%. No fewer than one-quarter of all new alcohol brands launched in the United States in the five years to 2007 were types of vodka. In the UK, where Scotch whisky and gin once reigned supreme, vodka is now pre-eminently the preferred spirit, with growth in the three years from 2009 forecast to be in the region of a further 20%.

In one sense, the only unexpected aspect to vodka's rise to kingpin status is that it took as long as it did. As we shall see when we trace vodka's surprising history in the pages that follow, it has been a presence in western markets since the period immediately after the Second World War. That obviously makes it very much the younger sibling of the other European grain and grape spirits, and yet it has taken half a century of steady growth to enshrine it in the unrivalled position it enjoys today. It is, paradoxically, at one and the same time precocious young upstart and late developer.

You might think that vodka's huge international following is based largely on the fact that most of it doesn't taste of anything, and indeed that was doubtless the principal driver of its early popularity. We shall discover though, as we embark on a world tour of vodka brands, from the long-established names to the new kids on the block, that vodka is an infinitely more nuanced and fascinating drink than earlier generations could ever have believed. And that growing realization, together with an understanding of its manifold possibilities as a drink, is now a significant factor in its worldwide market share.

Vodka is no longer solely the spirit for people who don't like the taste of spirits. There are vodkas made from wheat, rye, corn, barley, potatoes, even grapes. And that's before we've begun to consider those that are flavoured with anything from lemon to vanilla, apple to passionfruit, or boosted with caffeine or ginseng. There are pink vodkas, black vodkas, vodkas with blades of grass, ears of wheat or handfuls of raspberries bobbing about in them. In a market permanently agasp for the shock of the new, all this helps to make vodka the most dynamic spirits category there has ever been.

Nor is its production confined any longer to its traditional heartlands. Because it is in essence such a simple drink to make, requiring only a reliable source of grain (or other raw material) and good clean water, it is less geographically specific than any other distilled drink. There is, to be sure, a 'vodka belt' that stretches from western and southern Russia into Poland, the Baltic states and Scandinavia, but that doesn't stop enterprising producers from making it on the sun-soaked American west coast, in the English Home Counties, amid the Alpine foothills of northern Italy or in the rain-washed highlands of Mexico.

I have aimed to represent the global reach of this exciting spirit. There is naturally a preponderance of eastern European products in these pages (and if there are more Polish than Russian vodkas, that doesn't reflect any kind of cultural bias, more the fact that the Poles have been much quicker off the starting blocks with penetration of western markets than their bigger neighbour). But I'm equally proud of those countries represented by just one or two brands – New Zealand, Austria, India and many others – for bearing the torch in parts of the world where there had previously been no vodka-drinking, let alone vodka-making, tradition.

It's a brave new, deeply complex world. But take my hand and we're halfway there.

Stuart Walton

Part 1
Introduction
to vodka

HISTORY OF VODKA

V odka – ice-clear, snow-pure spirit of the frozen north. To a whole generation of drinkers, it is just one of many options. Mixed with fruit juices, tonic, cola, ginger beer or sometimes knocked back on its own in the Slavic style from tiny glasses frosty with condensation, vodka surely needs no introduction. It's what you drink before you can get your grown-up palate around Scotch or cognac. And at least until a new wave of flavoured vodkas began to break upon the scene in the 1980s, it was not thought to demand any connoisseurial appreciation, for the starkly simple, crystal-clear reason that it didn't smell or taste of anything. Vodka is just… vodka.

Above: 'At the Cocktail Party', fashion plate from *Art Gout Beauté* magazine, 1927. The cocktail party became the most fashionable form of social gathering in the 1920s, as witness these elegant young things.

It might come as something of a surprise, therefore, to the cocktail crowd ordering up another pitcher of bracing Sea Breeze, that their grandparents' generation wouldn't have known what they were talking about. As recently as the 1950s, vodka was virtually unknown in the West. Its name might have cropped up in Russian novels. There was a certain idea gleaned from historical movies that it was something that Russian cavalry officers gulped down from silly little glasses, which were then smashed by being flung at the fireplace as though in contempt. But nobody in the West had ever actually come across it. Indeed, glass-flinging wasn't the kind of behaviour you wanted at a convivial soirée.

By the time vodka did reach western Europe in the 1920s, it hardly became an overnight sensation. The French had an array of traditional spirits of their own, while Americans drank whiskey and the British preferred either Scotch or gin. A more vigorous attempt to market it in the United States after the Second World War quickly ran aground in the inauspicious political climate of the period. With the nuclear arms race heralding the onset of the Cold War, vodka was inescapably the staple drink of the enemy, the engine fuel of communism, all the more sinister for looking and tasting like nothing in particular.

Its first aficionados were inevitably the dissident young, California beatniks and Parisian existentialists, people whose rejection of the culture of their elders meant forgoing honest southern bourbon or *fine champagne* cognac. Where the traditional spirits encouraged relaxed, post-prandial sipping, or were the bases for the staid, pre-dinner mixed drinks that were all that was left of the original cocktail era ('Gin and tonic, darling?'), vodka acquired at the outset of its western career an aura of non-conformist recklessness, and an association with youth that it sustained through to the dawn of the alcopop era.

Origins of vodka

When and where did vodka first appear? In the case of such a simple spirit, it is inevitably hard to tell. At what point does any distillate from a grain mash, a by-product of beer-brewing perhaps, start to take on an identity of its own, with its own terminology and special methods of preparation? Written records are very scarce. If only a sealed earthenware vessel from the medieval era would turn up during an archaeological excavation, and be found to contain some clear liquor that was recognizably a grain spirit, we might be on surer ground, but no such vessel has ever come to light. What we are left with instead is a nationalistic argument between the Russians and the Poles, a debate that became more heated toward the end of the Cold War era, when the two countries were still officially allies.

The name vodka is derived from the old Slavonic word for water, *voda*. There is a tradition in the Russian language of applying diminutive forms to familiar words, and *vodka* is the diminutive of *voda*, as are *vodonka* and *vodochka*. The notion is rather more of an endearment, though, than a belittling, so if we think of the translation as 'little water', implying that we are diminishing its impact and not quite taking it seriously, we are some way off the mark. It's more accurate to think of it along the lines of describing somebody who likes their food as being 'quite the little gourmet', or somebody pleasing on the eye as being a 'little stunner'. It implies that they are the distilled essence of whatever property it is they have, which is the relation of vodka to *voda*.

There is a strong linguistic tradition in the West of referring to distilled spirits by some variation on the phrase 'water of life'. This dates from the European origins of distillation in northern Italy and southern France around the turn of the thirteenth century. The extraction of an ardent liquor from the more familiar forms of grain beer, grape wine or fermented honey were conceived in alchemical terms as being a matter of isolating the soul – or indeed the 'spirit', hence the terminology – of intoxicating drinks. The belief was that this spirit would have life-prolonging, or at the very least medicinal, qualities, and so it came to be known in Latin as *aqua vitae*, water of life. This passed into many of the contemporary European languages to denote clear distillates of one form or another. In French it was *eau de vie*, in the Scandinavian languages it became variations on *aquavit/akvavit* and so forth, and in Scots Gaelic it was *uisge beatha*, from which is derived the word whisky.

While it is tempting to connect the 'water' derivation of vodka to this development, things are not quite that straightforward. The early Slavonic languages were not permeated by Latin. On the other hand, an important influence on the evolution of distillation in the Slavic countries occurred when, in 1386, an ambassador from the Genoese colony of Cafta in southeast Europe paid a visit to the court at Lithuania, which had lately converted to Catholicism, and brought with him a quantity of southern European *aqua vitae*. In a culture used to drinking nothing stronger than matured mead or ale, this was considered much too fiery to be a drink, and became initially a medicinal aid. Even then, it was diluted, and it may have been this practice that fixed its association with *voda* in these early times. Coming from a culture associated with wine production such as the Genoese, we can be fairly certain that this would have been a grape, as opposed to grain, spirit.

Indigenous production of a clear spirit began in the following century. Two existing factors probably contributed to the development of distillation techniques. One was that accidental occurrence of weak distillation may well have happened during the production of beer and mead. Fermented products were made by a very slow process over the course of the year. The first batch of beer made to celebrate the new year (which, in those days, was 1st March) would be strong, thick and full-flavoured. As the first beer was drawn off, more water would be added to what was left in the pot to continue the fermentation, and with each successive addition of water, the resulting brew grew weaker. The earthenware pot in which the beer or mead fermented was generally placed over a wooden tub to catch anything that boiled over, the heat beneath the pot being maintained at a more or less even temperature. Anything that dribbled into the tub beneath might occasionally have been pure alcohol driven off the fermenting brew.

Another factor that surely influenced the development of distillation was the extraction of pitch. Pitch was used to make boats and wooden barrels impermeable, and also in the foundations and roofs of dwellings. Pine and birch wood was burned in a cast-iron stove, which was fitted with channels to allow the pitch to drain out. Alternatively, it was boiled in water, with pipes fitted to the top of the cauldron, in which the pitch condensed to a liquid as it cooled. The idea of driving out some essential element contained within the wood, or indeed within the beer or mead, and collecting it in pipes for later use, was already a perfected technique.

Distillation techniques appear to have developed gradually among Russian monastic communities during the early part of the fifteenth century. A key event may have been the delegation that the state of Moscow sent to the Ecumenical Councils of the Catholic Church in the late 1430s. They travelled through Italy over two to three years, visiting four major city-states, including Florence and Venice, and would have encountered the *aqua vitae* that western

Above: 'Catherine the Great of Russia' (1729–1796) by Fyodor Stepanovich Rokotov, 1770, now in the Hermitage museum, St Petersburg. Catherine was an assiduous promoter of Russian culture, including the appreciation of fine vodka, to the crowned heads and famous names of Europe.

monasteries produced from grape wine. They would have been fascinated by both the drink and the apparatus used in its production. Pot distillation, in which the vapour driven off the heated wine is collected in a condenser and then subjected to further distillation, would not have been that hard to grasp, and must have been easy to apply back home. The only difference was that the Russian monks would have to work with a grain-based alcohol such as ordinary beer or the regional speciality, kvass (rye beer).

Vodka – but not as we know it

In these early times, distilled grain spirits varied enormously. Quality depended on how many distillations the raw material had been subjected to, and how efficiently – if at all – it had been filtered. Batches of alcohol made from the first and last stages of the distilling process, which are full of those impurities known as congeners, would have smelled and tasted foul. The effects of drinking them were legendarily ghastly, but the aroma and taste at least could be masked by additives such as herbs, spices, fruits, berries, hops, wormwood and so forth. These were the forerunners of the traditional flavoured vodkas. In due course, distillation spread from the monasteries outwards into the homes of peasant families.

A state monopoly on spirit production was in existence by the 1470s, promulgated by Tsar Ivan III; the earliest example of the state control of distillation, this provides strong circumstantial evidence that it had begun to flourish in the area of Moscow before it had taken root in any of the surrounding territories. The Church was permitted to produce vodka for its own purposes until the seventeenth century, until this too was outlawed by state decree.

In the eighteenth century, the state gave up its monopoly. The first recorded use of the word vodka as a drink – rather than as an antiseptic for dressing wounds or as a medicinal tincture – appears in an official document of 1751. This was a decree of the Tsarina Elizabeth I entitled 'Who is to be Permitted to Possess Vats for the Distillation of Vodkas'.

In common parlance, the term 'vodka' began to take hold quite widely from the era of Catherine the Great's reign (1762–1796) onwards. Oddly, however, it was reserved, with qualifiers, for the aromatized versions of the drink. In Aleksandr Pushkin's verse novel *Eugene Onegin* (1825–1832), for example, the term *russkaia vodka* refers specifically to a spirit flavoured with anise. The clear, plain spirit we know most familiarly as vodka was referred to by some variation on the phrase 'distilled wine' (*varenoe vino*), 'grain wine' (*khlebnoe vino*) or 'burning wine' (*goriashchi vino*).

Getting into the (Russian) spirit

Western appreciation of vodka only really took off in the latter part of the eighteenth century, during the reign of Tsarina Catherine II, known to history as Catherine the Great. Catherine was a doughty promoter of Russian culture, as well as having distinctly western-oriented intellectual tastes. She met and corresponded with many of the great names of the day in science, philosophy and literature, and was herself a connoisseur of vodka. Following her edict of 1765, a licence to distil could only be held by members of the landed gentry. Noble families such as the Kurakins and Razumovskys went into the business of rivalling each other to produce ever finer and smoother types of vodka, some of which were fervently deemed to outshine anything that Cognac had to offer.

Catherine sent a consignment of vodka to the famously unimpressible French writer and philosopher Voltaire, author of *Candide* and patriotic wine-lover. She sent it to her fellow European reigning monarchs, including Gustav III of Sweden and Frederick the Great of Prussia, men who must have tasted clear grain spirit many times before, but who were duly impressed by the enormous advances in quality that were now being achieved. The drink won friends among writers such as the German poet and novelist Johann Wolfgang von Goethe and the philosopher Immanuel Kant, the Swiss scientist Johann Kaspar Lavater, and perhaps most famously of all, the great Swedish natural scientist Carl Linnaeus, founder of the botanical and zoological classification system that bears his name.

Linnaeus was given vodka on a trip to Russia in the 1760s, and was so impressed that he wrote a treatise in praise of it, one that has been much quoted by Russian distillers ever since. 'This drink has a magical power,' he wrote. 'It strengthens the weak, and revives those who have fainted. Those tired after work and physical activity can return their life forces by this drink much sooner than by nourishment.' He was convinced it had a formidable range of medical and gastronomic applications. 'It works as a diuretic, an appetizer, an anti-toxin.' In short, it was something between a magic potion and a cure-all.

Wars are often the chief engines of cultural transplantation, as the movements of armies carry new habits and tastes to and from the

Below: Dmitri Mendeleev (1834–1907) established the optimum proportions of alcohol to water in vodka, setting the industry standard.

combat zones where they are posted. It was the Thirty Years' War of the seventeenth century, for example, that is held to have brought the taste for gin to England from the Low Countries. Similarly, the mass European mobilization that accompanied the Napoleonic Wars in the early years of the nineteenth century saw Russian soldiers being sent to many different parts of the continent. Almost wherever they went, they brought vodka with them, helping to popularize the rougher and readier versions of the drink among the ordinary strata of society, where the crowned heads, poets and philosophers had enjoyed the crème de la crème.

Vodka became the officially accepted term for a clear spirit in the late nineteenth century, when it was once again subsumed under state monopoly. In 1894, an official standard for the production and composition of vodka was promulgated by the Russian government. It was based on chemical experiments conducted by the celebrated scientist Dmitri Mendeleev (1834–1907), who was appointed director of the Imperial Bureau of Weights and Measures in 1893. Mendeleev established what the ideal proportions of spirit and water should be in vodka. These were 38% ethyl alcohol to 62% water. The official definition of vodka was henceforth that it was a grain spirit, triple-distilled and then diluted with water down to an alcohol level of 40% by volume (rounded up from Mendeleev's 38% to simplify the tax calculation). This was further codified into law in 1902, and became the only permissible formula for what was by then known patriotically as Moscow vodka, to distinguish it from any rivals.

Western emigration and Eastern decline

In the 1860s, a distillery was founded in Moscow by one Piotr Smirnov. It was a quality operation, and appears to have been the first to use the technique of charcoal-filtering the spirit as standard. This resulted in a product that was seen as sufficiently pure and refined to be adopted by royal warrant, and in 1886 the Smirnov family became official purveyors to the Romanov court. Piotr, the founder, died in 1910, and was succeeded at the helm of the business by his third son, Vladimir. All was well until the great upheaval of October 1917, when the revolutionary Bolshevik government confiscated the premises and closed down the distillery. Lenin, the first leader of Soviet Russia, had long believed that vodka was one of the factors holding back working people's emancipation, and that if they were to be free to realize their potential and build the world's first socialist state, vodka prohibition was unavoidable.

Vladimir Smirnov was denounced as having conspired with the deposed imperial authorities to befuddle the masses with intoxicating liquor, arrested, and imprisoned by a revolutionary tribunal. He was sentenced to death as an enemy of the people. In circumstances that remain shrouded in mystery, he escaped and fled the country southward into Turkey. By 1920, he had re-established the family distillery in Constantinople (modern-day Istanbul). Four years later, amid the turbulent events that led to the founding of the modern state of Turkey, Smirnov moved production of his vodka to the then Polish city of Lwow (now Lviv in Ukraine). Opening a second production facility in Paris the following year, he altered the spelling of the product to Smirnoff, which is how the name is rendered in French.

Smirnoff vodka prospered relatively well in its new western home, at least until the onset of the worldwide economic depression of the 1930s. In 1933, Smirnov took the biggest decision of his entrepreneurial life, and sold the brand to another Russian emigré, Rudolf Kunett. Kunett moved the production to the United States, which at the time was only just recovering from the 13-year disaster that had been national liquor Prohibition. In due course, Kunett sold the brand on to a company called Heublein, but the extraordinary trajectory was already complete. By means largely of the inspired tenacity of a single refugee, vodka had emigrated from its Russian homeland, via western Europe, to the United States, and thus set up camp all over the western world.

Ironically, meanwhile, in the Soviet Union of the 1930s, Lenin's successor Stalin completely rethought the official Bolshevik line on distilled spirits, and reintroduced vodka production under state monopoly. Formidable production targets were set, and the standard strength was increased in the direction of 50%. Historians have suggested that Stalin's enthusiastic encouragement of vodka consumption was driven by much the same reasons for which Lenin had once excoriated it – that it kept the masses too stupefied to protest at the actions of their political masters.

Whatever the risks of stupefaction, vodka was issued as a ration to Russian soldiers throughout the Second World War (much as British sailors were once issued with rum), and became so much a part of the culture that servicemen who took to it with anything less than the instinctual enthusiasm of ducks to water were viewed with suspicion as lacking true comradely *esprit de corps*. The practice certainly did much to undermine the communist puritanism with regard to alcohol of the early Leninist days. Dysfunctional drinking has often been seen as an ingrained aspect of the Russian use of vodka, with public drunkenness and brawling having been a feature of the urban landscape since at least the latter part of the eighteenth century. Those who view this as

Above: Russian anti-alcohol poster of the 1920s, reading: 'The Cost. A final warning.'

integral to the Russian national character, though, are guilty of a condescending generalization.

A Russian researcher, William Pokhlebkin, argued in an important work of 1991 that the degree of public drunkenness in Russian society has been directly related to whether a state monopoly on the production and sale of vodka is in place at any given moment. Vodka monopolies are a feature of the strong, stable regimes in that country's history. It is often only when domestic politics has been disturbed by economic or constitutional crises that the monopoly has been surrendered, as was the case when Catherine the Great ceded the exclusive rights of production to the gentry in the late eighteenth century. As the profit motive drives prices up, people turn to illicitly distilled, potentially toxic products that are available in greater quantities, and the result has been civil disorder. For this reason alone, vodka is of deep-rooted interest to social historians as an accurate indicator of the health of society.

In the 1980s, the Soviet Union's last president, Mikhail Gorbachev, instituted a stringent anti-alcoholism campaign that closed down the state distilleries and encouraged people to drink beer or wine instead. The campaign had largely the opposite effect to what was intended, and failed because, as Pokhlebkin observes, it lacked a focused educative element. When the mass

of the population drank alcohol not, as he puts it, 'sitting at a table, but holding on to a lamp-post', what was needed was an appreciation of the correct gastronomic approach to the Russian national drink. Seeking to banish it altogether was to repeat the calamitous errors of the US legislators who introduced Prohibition in their country in 1919. And in Boris Yeltsin, Gorbachev's successor and the first elected president of the post-Soviet period, the Russian people were confronted with a national leader who, whatever his other achievements, turned out visibly to have proved quite impervious to all the anti-vodka propaganda.

Above: Harry MacElhone, left, mixes a cocktail at Harry's New York Bar, Paris, in 1949. He bought the place in 1923.

Mixing it

Vodka's most notable appearance in the West in the generation prior to its commercial takeoff in the 1950s was in the Bloody Mary cocktail, which had first seen the light of day at Harry's New York Bar in Paris in the aftermath of the First World War. It was said to have been invented by a barman called Fernand Petiot, in honour of one of his customers, a lovelorn Mary who haunted the bar each evening nursing an unrequited love. Not only would the vodka itself have been a commercial novelty at this time, but so too was the tomato juice that gave it its gory colour. The Bloody Mary has weathered the years with remarkable tenacity, and is correctly thought to be a thoroughly nutritious drink. Its reputation as a hangover soother derives partly from its vitamin-packed goodness, partly from the spicy kick of Worcestershire sauce, Tabasco and pepper (the combination of which theoretically gives the churning stomach something else to think about), and partly from the fact that the hair-of-the-dog slug of alcohol it contains is so comprehensively disguised by the other ingredients.

As an exotic and hard-to-come-by import, vodka makes the odd tentative appearance in the *Savoy Cocktail Book* of 1930, the era's definitive route-map to serious drinking. A cocktail simply called Russian comprised equal, jarring measures of vodka, gin and chocolate liqueur, and may be thought of as the antecedent of the popular Black Russian of the 1980s cocktail revival, which mixed vodka with Tia Maria and cola. The association of vodka with chocolate seems to have been fixed in this early period. A mixture of vodka with white chocolate liqueur and cream was named after a long-forgotten lady named Barbara. Blue Monday, meanwhile, was vodka and Cointreau with blue food colouring in it (an original touch in an age when blue curaçao was not yet heard of).

Below: An early reference to vodka being used for cocktails in the *Savoy Cocktail Book* of 1930. The mixture isn't a particularly elegant one.

COCKTAILS

⅓ Crème de Cacao. ⅓ Dry Gin. ⅓ Vodka. *Shake well, strain into cock-tail glass, and tossitoff quickski.*	RUSSIAN COCKTAIL.
1 Dash Angostura Bitters. 4 Dashes Syrup. 1 Glass Rye or Canadian Club Whisky. *Stir well and strain into cock-tail glass. Add 1 cherry.*	RYE WHISKY COCKTAIL.
The Juice of ½ Lemon and ¼ Grapefruit. The White of 1 Egg. 1 Liqueur Glass Green Chartreuse. *Shake well and strain into cocktail glass.*	ST. GERMAIN COCKTAIL.

An attempt to translate : " This hooch is the Cat's Pyjamas," from North American into fluent Russian.

Even if vodka was available in chic cocktail bars, however, it would be another 20 years or more before it became a staple tipple in pubs and in the home. One of the most obvious mixers for a clear spirit is orange juice, and in the 1950s, the Screwdriver – essentially a straightforward vodka-and-orange, usually with a pinch of sugar – was born. It is said to have acquired its name from the fact that it had become a favourite drink of American oil-rig workers, one of whom enterprisingly used a screwdriver one day to stir the ingredients together – a more manly alternative, perhaps, to the silver swizzle stick of the pre-war cocktail crowd.

By the time of the great cocktail renaissance of the 1980s, vodka was firmly established as a cocktail ingredient. In its neutral guise, it gave an extra kick to a fruity mixture, and its lack of both flavour and colour made it a natural back-

Above: Sean Connery as James Bond in *Dr No*, 1962. Bond's preference for a vodka martini –
'shaken not stirred' – is established in this, the first Bond movie.

ground component for a drink that highlighted more exotic ingredients, such
as liqueurs flavoured with tropical fruits like melon, passionfruit or banana,
or those with head-turning colours, like the achingly trendy blue curaçao.
When the new-fangled flavoured vodkas started hitting the market in the late
1980s, the sky was the limit. Flavoured vodka has to a great extent elbowed
aside the old traditional fruit-based liqueurs on cocktail menus. Not only is it
less syrupy in texture, but it represents a more streamlined approach. To
choose a random example, with blackcurrant-flavoured Absolut Kurant
available, the bartender no longer needs to add cassis (blackcurrant liqueur)
to ordinary vodka; it also provides a purple fruit flavour without the murky
colour of crème de cassis.

WHERE VODKA IS MADE

Traditional vodka-producing countries

The distilled grain spirit that came to be known as vodka first emigrated into the territories immediately surrounding the Moscow state in the fifteenth and sixteenth centuries. These were broadly the regions that comprised the grain-growing belt that encompasses Poland, Lithuania, Ukraine, Belarus, and the western Russian principalities such as Novgorod, Tver, Ryazan and Nizhniy Novgorod, which have long since been absorbed into greater Russia. For various reasons, to do with such issues as shortage of grain, war and siege, and lack of comparable contacts with western expertise in distillation, none of the western principalities could have developed the technique of grain spirit distillation before Moscow itself. As to the other countries – both Poland and those that, until 1991, fell within the ambit of greater Russia – there are no extant records or evidence to place the origins of a precursor to vodka as early as the circumstantial evidence places it in Moscow.

Nonetheless, these were the first territories to which the techniques and expertise were transported, and they all soon developed grain spirit traditions of their own. An interesting point about the rudimentary forms of vodka that came to be developed here is that their names often derive from linguistic roots denoting 'burning'. These include: *gorzalka* (Polish), *gorilka* (Ukrainian), *garelka* (Belorussian) and *degtiné* (Lithuanian). The dual implication of these terminologies is that the spirit itself was ardent (from the Latin for burning) and ready to catch light easily, and also that when poured down the throat, burning was the most accurate description of the effect it produced. It should be remembered that, in these early times, the strongest alcohol anybody had previously drunk would have been matured beer or mead, which might attain a strength of about 15% alcohol (something like today's pale dry sherry) if it was allowed slowly to continue fermenting.

Spirit distillation emerged partly independently in the Scandinavian countries, which had their own monastic traditions. The earliest surviving record we have of Russian vodka being exported was to Sweden in 1505. A political alliance between Poland and Sweden in the later sixteenth century led to some cross-fertilization of techniques in spirit production between the two kingdoms, but in other countries, distillation pursued a separate path. As in the poorer regions bordering Moscow, grain harvests were often too unreliable to provide enough of a surplus for distillation. After their introduction to Europe in the late sixteenth century, potatoes gradually became a cheaper option; as well as being used in vodka to this day, they are still the basis for some of the variations on aquavit produced around the Baltic and in Germany. Norwegian aquavit, for example, is a potato-based spirit, flavoured with caraway and/or dill. Aquavit has always been flavoured with these aromatizing elements, whereas aromatized vodka was only one sub-type of a fundamental spirit that was developing in the direction of ultra-refined neutrality and purity of flavour.

Vodka and its variants remained an eastern European speciality throughout the sixteenth and seventeenth centuries. Western Europe had its whiskies, its cognac and armagnac, dark, richly flavoured, cask-aged distillates made from either grain mash or grape wine, as well as Dutch genever (the ancestor of England's gin). Artisanal production of ardent spirits distilled from fruits, such as the various *eaux de vie* of France, Normandy's calvados (apple brandy), Germany's and Switzerland's kirsch (from cherries), continued to diversify, but there was nothing comparable to the clear grain spirit of eastern Europe. And even within the so-called vodka belt of north-east Europe, a marked divergence between the Russian and Polish-Lithuanian styles was to arise. While the latter favoured richness and aromatic character, the Russians headed in the direction of perfecting an ever purer, more fastidiously neutral, flavour-free spirit.

It was only in the twentieth century, with the journey in exile of Vladimir Smirnov, as we have seen, and the subsequent export of the formula to the United States, that vodka began to acquire a global reputation and put down roots far from its original homeland. It is now made all over the world, sometimes under local licence by the eastern European companies. Much is still produced in the former states of the USSR, but other products originate from a diverse range of countries, from Mexico to New Zealand.

Above: Potatoes arriving at a distillery in Poland. While most vodka nowadays is based on grain, potatoes are still used by a number of specialist producers.

HOW VODKA IS MADE

G iven that classic plain vodka is such a simple drink, you could be forgiven for thinking that there can't be too much to the formula for making it. If Russian peasants could knock it up at home in conditions of dire poverty, surely anybody can do it? The point is, however, that those home distillates were noxious substances that had a dreadful effect on their unlucky consumers. Real vodka, even when produced to the minimum industry standard, involves much greater care in its manufacture.

The main ingredient

One myth which still holds surprisingly wide currency is that most vodka is made from potatoes. Vodka is, in fact, more usually a grain distillate, made from rye, wheat, barley, maize (corn), millet, oats, or some combination of those cereals. On its home turf in Russia, until the late nineteenth century, rye was the predominant, if not exclusive, grain used. The other component that found its way into traditional Russian vodka was a tiny admixture to the basic rye mash of other grains, residues from farming procedures such as milling and grinding. These might be the bran husks removed from wheat, flakes of oats, and frag-ments of barley, buckwheat or cracked wheat grains, all of which would constitute no more than about 1–1.5% of the total grain mash, but which would nonetheless contribute a more complex character to the finished spirit. While some brands still use only rye, wheat became a more widespread ingredient in the twentieth century. Sugar-cane molasses are another common base nowadays. Sugar beet is generally frowned on as the lowest of the low.

For centuries potatoes have generally been the recourse of only the poorest families, or in times of general economic difficulty. It is popularly believed in Russia that potato spirit is more likely to give you a horrible hangover than thoroughly rectified grain spirit, and even, more mythically, that potato spirit is more likely to make the user aggressive under its influence. Since it would be difficult to know how to test that hypothesis, we can perhaps only note it and back gingerly away from anyone who has had a skinful of potato hooch.

Facing page: above left rye, the original Russian vodka grain; **above right** wheat, now the principal crop for vodka, growing here in Altai, Siberia; **below left** six-row barley, much favoured for Scandinavian vodkas; **below right** many North American vodkas are made from corn (maize).

Water

Of equal importance to the grain is a supply of good-quality water, the ingredient that, after all, gives vodka its name. Classically, this has always been pure, free-running river water with low mineral hardness. In Russia, that water is now sourced from the streams of the Moscow and Neva rivers, in particular the soft, clear water of the Vazuza tributary of the former, where it runs through dense forest in the Smolensk province to the west of the city of Moscow. In the eighteenth century, when the private distillers were competing to outdo each other on quality, the water was sourced from the Mytishchi springs around 20 km (12 miles) outside the city, which had been set up as the main water supply for Moscow. The water is further purified before use by being filtered through layers of sand, and then having pure oxygen bubbled through it. Only then is it fit to be an ingredient in the production of quality vodka.

Not all vodka producers are able to rely on spring water or pure river water for their manufacture. Where they aren't, the recourse is generally to purify the water by distilling it. This is achieved by the same method as alcohol distillation: by heating it and then collecting the condensed matter that runs off. As the steam from the heated water hits a cold surface, it reliquefies and runs off

Above: Ice floes on Lake Vättern in Sweden, home of Svensk Vodka. Quite a few premium vodkas use glacial meltwater in their composition.

Fig. 2. — Appareils de mélange à l'eau pour obtenir l'eau-de-vie.
Filtres à charbon et à sable.

Above: An engraving by Louis Poyet in *La Nature* showing vodka being distilled in Russia in 1901. This engraving shows the mixing apparatus to obtain the spirit before it is filtered through carbon and sand. Aspects of the distillery design remain recognizable today.

as water, but now with rather less of its mineral content than it originally had. For those grades of spirit where even this is too much of an investment, the last resort is simply to boil the water and reuse it. This at least will liberate some of the impurities in it. Purists will insist that no quality vodka can be made with distilled or boiled water. Distilled water has a lifeless, flat taste compared to spring water, a claim that isn't hard to verify by home experiment.

Distillation

Vodka begins, like beer, as a fermented grain mash. The grains are induced to germinate and sprout by soaking them in water. These sprouted grains are roasted to bring out their natural sugars, then crushed and mixed with water; the sugars provoke an alcoholic fermentation in the grain gruel when it is heated. This fermented liquid is then subjected to repeated distillations, during which an ever purer alcoholic residue is condensed out by the continuous application of heat.

The first and last parts of the spirit that are driven off are where most of the congeneric substances – fusel-oil, aldehydes and ethyl acetate, compounds that add flavour to a spirit but can contribute to its raw or unclean taste – are concentrated. These will be discarded. Congeners add character to spirits such as whisky, brandy and rum, but in a neutral spirit such as vodka, where there will be no other flavour-influencing element, such as cask-aging, to balance them out, they are most definitely not wanted.

In a process known as rectification, some of the liquid is fed back from the condenser on to a series of plates where the rising vapour is passing. They interact so that some of the vapour liquefies, and some of the distilled liquid vaporizes, in effect creating a redistillation.

The more distillation cycles the drink undergoes, the purer and stronger is the ethyl alcohol that results. For some premium products, the process continues until the strongest possible spirit is reached (about 96% pure). Compare this to, say, cognac, where the spirit is distilled until it reaches a little above its final bottled strength. It may come off the still at 50%, and then be adjusted down to 40% for bottling. Vodka is to all intents and purposes the *ne plus ultra* of the distiller's art. It is much closer to pure alcohol, and is only brought down to its bottled strength of 40–45% (or 37.5% for the standard western brands) by the addition of that all-important water before bottling.

Charcoal filtration

There is one final ingredient in the production of quality plain vodka, and that is charcoal. When the distilled spirit runs out of the condenser, it is subjected to a rigorous filtration to remove as much of its impurity as possible. Toward the end of the eighteenth century, it was established that a layer of charcoal was much the best medium for this task. Prior to that, anything from cotton cloth to crushed stone had been used to filter the spirit, but nothing succeeded quite as efficiently as wood charcoal. To best activate the wood, the outer bark is removed, as is any darker wood from close to the core of the trunk, and hard knots are excised.

The woods of certain trees are favoured: these have included birch, beech, lime, oak, alder, pine, fir, aspen and poplar, but overwhelmingly the most traditional in eastern European vodka production is birch, which combines high absorbent capacity with relative economy of production.

Other methods of purification have included chemical treatments such as the addition of bicarbonate of soda, as well as the use of foodstuffs such as egg white, milk and even sippets of traditional black bread, which trapped the contaminants within their mass for easy removal. In earlier times, some producers borrowed clarification techniques from wine- and beer-making, such as the use of expensive isinglass (the dried swim-bladder of the sturgeon), to which alcohol impurities stick like limpets, as well as chilling and/or freezing, to separate them out. None of these techniques is quite as efficacious as charcoal filtration, though, and indeed charcoal is often employed in the distillation of other fine spirits, such as American bourbon, to achieve a smooth-tasting drink that doesn't jar the palate with uncouth off-flavours.

Adding flavour

As we shall discover, a whole range of other flavouring elements can be added after distillation if the intention is not to produce a neutral vodka. These have included a wide assortment of herbs, spices, berries, fruit extracts, honey, even unsweetened chocolate, and represent various ways of making a virtue of necessity. When the technology wasn't available to purify the spirit thoroughly, flavourings were a useful recourse for masking its roughness and rankness.

A tiny quantity of sugar is often added to create a softer texture.

Above: Copper pot stills of this traditional design have been making a comeback in recent years in the production of speciality vodkas.

TYPES OF VODKA

Everyday brands of vodka are intended to be as neutral-tasting as is consonant with the laws of chemistry. They don't taste of nothing at all, since – as we shall see later – ethyl alcohol itself has a taste. If it didn't, vodka really would just taste of water. At its most basic, you can expect that the cheap corner-store brand you buy for chugging back with ice and a mixer will have been double-distilled and subjected to two filtrations. A small amount of vodka is produced without charcoal filtration, but this is because the manufacturer wants it to retain some distillation character, as opposed to being squeaky-clean, which is what the everyday consumer expects in a proprietary vodka.

Premium vodka

Most of the big brands offer premium bottlings alongside their market-leading label. These are generally slightly higher in alcohol than the standard grades (40%, as against the western norm of 37.5%), so the extra price may be buying nothing more than another couple of degrees of spirit – or a little less water, depending on how you look at it.

More usually, there is some claim to more refined treatment in the distillery, perhaps quadruple distillation or triple filtration. Others stress the use of speciality equipment, such as historically old copper pot stills, or gourmet ingredients like Polish silver birch charcoal or a particularly pure, low-mineral source of spring water. Filtration through precious-stone residues such as crushed garnet or even diamond dust have been sighted. Organically grown grain is the boast of at least one British brand, while barley-based Finlandia is blended with glacial meltwater so utterly pure that it requires neither demineralization nor charcoal filtration.

The differences between everyday vodka and the premium brands become crystal clear when the vodkas are tasted comparatively. In the higher grades, there is a softness and smoothness to the spirit, as one would expect, paradoxically belying the higher alcohol, and as they slip down the throat, there is a finishing touch of sweetness. If you then move back to tasting the standard grade, you will notice a harder catch to the alcohol, something rougher around the edges, and a distinct air of the chemistry laboratory. The rawer the spirit, the more medicinal it tastes. Of course, this is not to say that even basic brands of vodka are anything like the rough-and-unready products of home distillation – but the next time somebody says there is no point in paying the extra for a premium brand, you will be able to correct them.

There is an economic issue here, to be sure, but the analogy I use is with the question of bottled versus tap water. Objecting to the ridiculous mark-ups on bottled water in a restaurant, you may well ask for a free jug of tap water. This makes financial sense, but don't try to pretend that there's no difference in the taste. The chlorine in the tap water stands out like a sore thumb when you're drinking it at the dinner table, which may well be why restaurants often add a slice of lemon. A glass of cold water from the tap at home on a hot day is perfectly refreshing, but to many it's even nicer if it has gone through a water filter.

The same applies to vodka. If you're smothering it with diet cola, what the hell? As a product to be appreciated on its own merits, however, it offers a world of difference between its standard and premium manifestations that is just waiting to be explored.

Traditional flavours

There are so many flavoured vodkas on the market now that it sometimes feels as though neutral vodka is itself gradually becoming the niche product. Flavoured vodkas originated from the need to mask the foul odour and taste of unrectified home-distilled spirit. As various recipes were developed, particular blends of ingredients held to have curative properties – especially herbs – came to be favoured.

From the earliest days of distillation in Europe, spirit production has always gone hand in hand with medicine, whether as a simple but effective disinfectant for wounds, or more speculatively as a health-preserving elixir to promote overall well-being. What could be more luxurious or beautiful to behold than a clear spirit with little flecks of real gold leaf floating about in it? But in centuries gone by, gold was thought to have medically beneficial properties: indeed, one of the founding fathers of distillation, the Provençal physician Arnold de Villeneuve (1240–1312), apparently restored Pope Clement V to health after prescribing him an infusion of gold speckles. In so

Above: Virtually every city in the world now boasts a range of chic and sophisticated cocktail bars, where the approach to mixing has become almost scientific in its rigour. This is the Fifth Floor bar at Harvey Nichols, London.

doing, he saved himself from the predatory attentions of the Inquisition. Two birds, one stone. The Polish brand Goldwasser, containing small flakes of gold, has been produced since at least 1598, when it was prized for its health benefits.

Some of the longer-standing, traditional flavoured vodkas of Russia and Poland include: *pertsovka/pieprzówka* (crushed black peppercorns and/or chilli peppers); *limonnaya/cytrynówka* (natural lemon extracts); *zubrovka/zubrówka* (bison grass); *vishnovka/wiśniówka* (cherries); and *krupnik* (honey).

Certain traditional vodkas have other alcohol added to them in modest quantities. Poland's Extra Zytnia contains apple brandy, Starka includes fortified Malaga wine, and a Russian product, Okhotnichya, has a dash of white port.

Modern flavours

From the late 1980s on, a new generation of flavoured vodkas began to appear on the international market. Initially, these reflected the traditional flavourings, but with a sweeter, less overwhelming degree of concentration. Pepper and lemon vodkas were easier to understand if they were just called that, and came with the reassurance of a brand that was already widely familiar. Swedish Absolut, a brand with its origins in the nineteenth century, was in the vanguard of this trend. Its Peppar bottling, containing essential oils of jalapeño chillies, was launched in 1986, and became a favoured ingredient for a really full-on Bloody Mary. It was followed in 1988 by Citron, which wasn't just lemon, but combined a fruit-basket of citrus flavours: mandarin, orange, lime and grapefruit. Over the following two decades, these have been joined by Kurant (blackcurrant), Mandrin (orange and mandarin), Vanilia, Raspberri, Apeach, Ruby Red (pink grapefruit), Pears and – in 2008 – Mango.

The flavour boom has meant that virtually all new vodka brands launching in the West now come in at least two or three flavours, as well as the neutral version. Citrus flavours are popular, as are pepper variations, and vanilla has proved a commercial winner. Other fruit flavourings have gone distinctly tropical, with mango, pineapple and melon, and there are journeys into the salad bowl, such as cucumber vodkas. Obscure herbal concoctions might have received an approving nod from Arnold de Villeneuve, the thirteenth-century French distiller, for all that he would never have heard of the Burmese black catechu that flavours and colours Blavod, the world's first black vodka, launched in 1996. For the truly intrepid, there is cannabis vodka from the Czech Republic, which contains sufficiently little of the active ingredient of cannabis, tetrahydrocannabinol, to allow it to dip under the EU regulation bar.

In short, the world has gone mad, but in a happy way. These products have inspired a whole new generation of cocktail recipes, because they mostly neither colour nor sweeten a mixture, but do possess the kinds of bracing fruit flavours that we expect to find in a long cold drink.

ENJOYING VODKA

Above: The Absolut Icebar at the Below Zero restaurant and lounge, London. Bars constructed from ice, maintained at around –5°C, have become an international design trend.

Until the most recent generation, few people understood quite how vodka was traditionally drunk. It became known as a cocktail ingredient, and then the simple basis for mixed drinks such as vodka-and-tonic and vodka-and-orange, drinks for people who weren't partial to the peculiar perfume of gin or the pungent edge of even the blandest brands of white rum. What has helped to orientate vodka appreciation along the lines of the cultures where it originated has, paradoxically, been its momentous spread across the globe.

Habitués of cocktail bars from Brighton to Baltimore may be shocked to learn of it, but to the inhabitants of Poznan or Podolsk, vodka-drinking is not primarily a matter of Sea Breezes and Woo-Woos. The drink has its own proper contexts, just as sherry or brandy do, some of them gastronomic, some of them celebratory, and we are missing out if we only ever see vodka as the basis for a mixed drink.

Vodka with food

The best use of vodka taken in its natural state is with food. There isn't much of a tradition of drinking spirits with food in the West, other than perhaps a dram of malt whisky with haggis in Scotland. We have absorbed the traditions of the European wine regions so deeply that drinking anything stronger than wine with food seems eccentric at best, and a grating mismatch

Above: Caviar on ice has long been a classic Russian combination with vodka, which should be served icy cold.

at worst. But just as the traditional dishes of viticultural Europe developed in harmony with their local wines – so that tomatoey red wines made in Tuscany go superbly well with tomato-based pasta dishes, or the light, acidic dry white wine of Muscadet is a surefire shoo-in with Brittany seafood – so the gastronomic cultures of Russia, Poland and the rest have evolved in symbiosis with vodka.

Russian zakuski are a prime example. Many gastronomic cultures around the world have some version of an array of small appetizers, nibbles, call them what you will. Scandinavia has its smörgasbord, Greece has meze. There is Indian thali, Chinese dim sum and Spanish tapas. Zakuski are Russia's answer to this custom. The word means something like 'little bites', and they come in many different guises. What links them all is that they are based on various methods of food preservation. During long northern winters, when fresh food was scarce or non-existent, domestic households traditionally relied on foods they had put by in the more benign months. Before the advent of home refrigeration, salting, smoking, pickling and drying were the chief techniques. Zakuski have salty, strong savoury or sour flavours, with high seasoning and often a spicy edge to them, from mustard or pepper. They can be meat, fish or vegetable, with fish providing the greatest variety of preparations.

Smoked herring, salted salmon, sturgeon prepared in any number of ways, from setting in aspic to hot- and cold-smoking, are all favourites. There are little sprats, Baltic whitefish, smelt from the saltwater lakes, and freshwater fish such as pike, as well as the cured roes of salmon and herring. One item that has achieved international renown is of course the pressed salted roe of the Russian sturgeon, otherwise known as caviar. Meat zakuski tend to be fatty, as fat is a good medium for preserving cooked food. They include pig brawn, jellied pork and ham, salt-cured beef, boiled and salted ox tongue, and strips of pure pork fat pickled in vinegar. More humble vegetable (and fruit) nibbles might encompass pickled cabbage and beetroot, marinated mushrooms, and an array of dry-salted items such as aubergine, water-melon, tomatoes, cucumber, even apples.

Alongside the zakuski, a Russian spread might also begin with little buckwheat pancakes known as blini, which may be eaten with black or pink caviar, smoked salmon, smetana (soured cream), or just butter. Solianka is a chunky, salty soup made from meat or fish, containing pickled cucumber or capers.

As we migrate westward along the Baltic, versions of these nibbles become the principal ingredients of larger dishes, with the reliably plentiful herring as the star of the show. Pickled and salted herring eaten with boiled potatoes, or spread with raw or marinated onion, or dressed in mustard or tomato sauces, feature strongly. Different ways of curing herring include the faintly terrifying northern Swedish *surströmming*, herring that is brined and fer-mented in cans, so that the tin buckles under the evolving gases and may explode when opened. *Lutefisk* from Finland, Norway and Sweden is dried whitefish that has been cured in lye (caustic soda). Meatballs of mixed pork and beef or veal are a classic Swedish dish, now often served as a canapé. Pastry dumplings or little pasties crop up all over northern and eastern Europe, from Poland's *pierogi* (*pirogi* in Russian), with cheese, mushroom, potato or cabbage fillings, to the generally meat-filled *pelmeni*.

What all these foods have in common is that they are most successfully accompanied by vodka. There are various reasons for this. One is the fact that the spirit strength of the drink acts to cut the fattiness that is a feature of many of these preparations; the same kind of effect is provided by the acidity in wine when paired with the fatty dishes of France and southern Europe. But fattiness is not the only story with these foods. Pickling brine and strong saltiness absolutely kill the flavours of wine, whereas the dry, clean, neutral impact of vodka holds up against them. Even certain smoked foods find it a more sympathetic partner. Then again, there is the fact that many of these dishes contain a grain element, in the form of pancakes or pastry, and a grain spirit makes a closer gustatory match with the food than a grape wine would.

The gastronomic refinement of vodka as an accompaniment to food arose in the eighteenth century, during the period when the drink itself was coming to be highly valued as a premium product in its homelands. While there had long been a tradition among the Russian aristocracy of drinking the fine wines of western Europe – great burgundy and Rhine wines in particular – the poor people knocked back whatever booze they could afford, in drinking sessions that often preceded, or entirely stood in for, the business of solid sustenance. In the later eighteenth century, a connoisseurial approach to vodka began to spread among the nobility who were now, after all, its chief producers. Serving vodka instead of wine to go with lavish banquets became a statement not just of patriotic fervour, but of competitive refinement as well.

Serving vodka

When serving vodka with food, it would obviously be inappropriate to take it in anything like the quantities in which wine is served. The bottle can be mercilessly chilled (you have the benefit of a domestic freezer that was unavailable to Prince Kurakin's household), and the drink served in small glasses no bigger than a shot-glass, or at most a little liqueur glass. Strictly speaking, the vodka should not be mixed with anything, nor have ice added to it, as it should be quite cold enough as it is. Needless to say, it should be taken in cautious, tiny sips. You will notice its alcohol strength on the palate interestingly mitigated both by the temperature at which it is served, and the highly seasoned foods it accompanies. Russian and Polish aficionados claim that if you approach it with respect in this way, situating it in its proper gastronomic context, you are much less likely to get drunk on it. That, naturally, depends on how much you get through, but the principle is undeniably a world away from just throwing it down by the double measure in a pub.

If you are looking for a digestif to relax with at the end of a vodka dinner, don't suddenly veer toward cognac, thereby risking a potentially calamitous collision of the grape and grain. This is where those traditional flavoured vodkas come into their own. Here, chilling is a matter of taste. There are those who feel that subjecting a fine bison-grass zubrówka to the indignity of the freezer is the act of a barbarian. A tangy cherry wiśniówka, on the other hand, is enhanced if it has been given the gentle chilling of a couple of hours in the fridge. Again, the aim is meditative, convivial sipping, not obliteration.

How to taste vodka

If you are setting about a comparative tasting of vodkas, or just want to examine the attributes of an individual vodka, there are a couple of simple principles to bear in mind.

First, the vodka should be well chilled. Give it a good swirl, to release the aromas – but remember these will be elusive or practically non-existent in some vodkas. Now, forget any wine-tasting you may have done. If you roll a mouthful of 40% spirit over your tongue, you'll soon know about it. In any case, you aren't looking for the same array of flavour characteristics. Vodka should be taken in a very small sip, which is retained at the front of the mouth, ideally with the head bent forward a little. If you want, you can draw a modicum of air over it, as you would when tasting a wine, but don't do that vigorous slurping you see wine people doing. Swallow it (or, if you're tasting more than one, spit it out) after a couple of seconds, rather than holding it in the mouth and dwelling on it. Its principal characteristics, such as how smooth the alcohol is, and whether it tastes sweet or harsh, can all be gleaned quite quickly.

Some people dilute spirits to taste, especially malt whisky, but there is no real point in weakening vodka. While a cask-aged spirit may be enhanced by a little water, vodka's aromatic subtleties will be drowned.

To experience the subtle differences between vodkas, you might like to compare three or four made from different ingredients: start with a wheat-based vodka, move on to a rye-based brand, and finish with a potato vodka. Taste lighter vodkas before those stronger in alcohol, and neutral vodkas before flavoured ones.

You will find, in the pages that follow, that we have discovered all kinds of herbal and spicy flavours even in the neutral vodkas. This isn't wishful thinking, since only pure water can taste and smell of nothing at all. Next time you open a bottle of your favourite brand of vodka, try tasting it in this way. You're bound to be surprised by the nuances and complexities it can offer – and you'll also be appreciating it in the way the drink's progenitors intended.

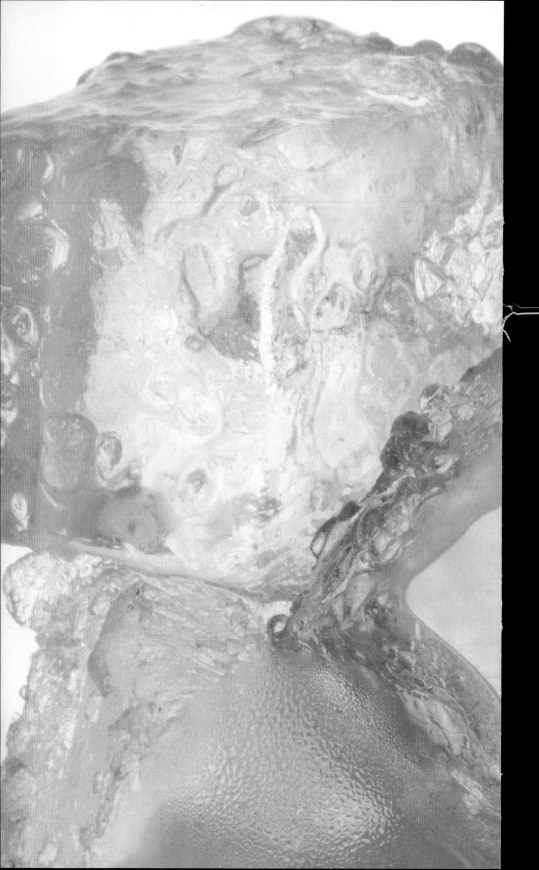

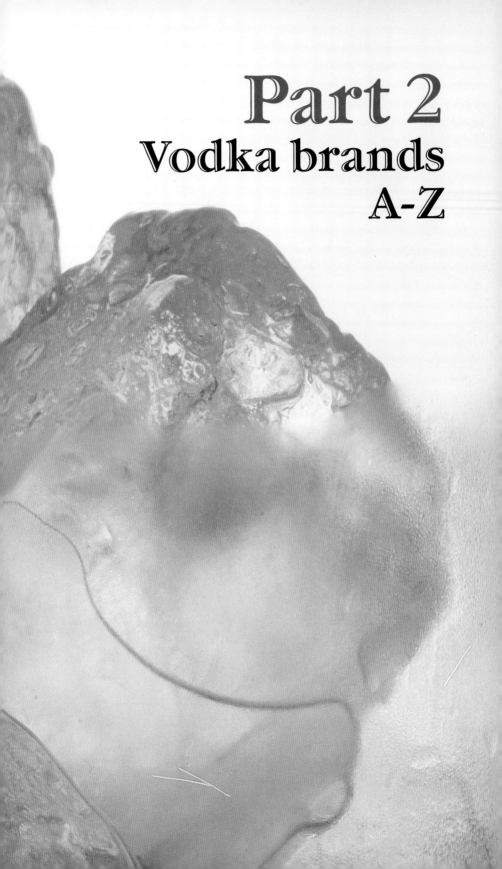

Part 2
Vodka brands
A-Z

42 BELOW

That magic number of 42 denotes not only the strength of the product, but also the fact that this vodka is made not far from the 42nd parallel south of the equator, in the world's most southerly distillery, just north of the New Zealand capital, Wellington. The country rightly prides itself on being a 'clean, green land', and it could only have been a matter of time before its world-class wine industry was supplemented by the production of a premium vodka.

Wheat grown under GM-free conditions is the base for 42 Below. The mash is distilled an initial three times, with extensive filtration, and then further purified with water from deep-lying springs 300 m (1000 feet) beneath an extinct volcano near the distillery. It is redistilled a fourth and final time before being bottled at slightly higher than the normal spirit strength.

The flavoured variants are appealingly original, with tropical fruits rather than citrus or berries. Feijoa, a green, wrinkly-skinned fruit originally native to South America and sometimes known as the pineapple guava, may not be familiar to many consumers. 42 Below Honey uses New Zealand's fabled manuka honey, produced from the pollen of the country's native tea tree (*Leptospermum scoparium*), long valued by the indigenous population for its medicinal properties.

A minimalist design approach has the brand name in white lettering on a clear bottle, with the flavour ID given in a small coloured panel.

Taste

There is a bracing, astringent quality to the nose of the neutral vodka, mildly suggestive of something medicinal. On entry, its gentle, caramel-soft spirit is immediately apparent, and there are faint herbal, even delicately floral, touches – perhaps fresh basil. All the time, you are aware of the discreet thrum of that 42% alcohol, which really does cleverly combine power with subtlety.

Passion has an expressive, precise scent of the juice of the passionfruit, very obviously fresh rather than anything confected, which passionfruit can so easily become. Sweet fruit notes are supported by a delicate herbal backnote,

Made from	Wheat, spring water
ABV	42%
Proof	84
Website	www.42below.com
Origin	New Zealand

and then the spirit comes barrelling through (but oh-so-gently) on the finish.

Kiwi (where else could it come from but New Zealand?) is also magically pure, juicy and enticing in its fruit impact.

Feijoa is the only 42 I find hard to love. There is a suggestion of pulpy guava to it, but there is a strongly medicinal, almost iodiney quality to the flavour that, to this palate at least, is asking to be overwhelmed with ginger beer or pineapple juice.

Honey has an aroma of thick, opaque, waxy honey, a palate that evokes stickily dripping honeycomb, and intriguing balance, in which the richness of the honey brilliantly offsets the smouldering spirit.

ABSOLUT

The Absolut success story is one to make producers of other spirit brands white-knuckled with envy. It has gone from strength to commercial strength in the past thirty years, and has achieved such widespread worldwide dissemination that it has been able to weather the economic storms that have seen other brands lose market share. 'Meteoric' is too small a word.

Much of this success has been built on market positioning. With its distinctive bottle design and a series of ad campaigns that have been imaginative without opting for niche elitism, not to mention a proliferating repertoire of modern, well-made flavour variants, it has captured the loyalties of a whole generation of vodka drinkers, those less concerned with historical background than with what goes into the coolest cocktails.

For all that, Absolut is a brand with heritage. It can trace its lineage back to 1879, when the redoubtable Lars Olsson Smith, Swedish politician and distiller, bestrode the world of Scandinavian spirit production like a colossus. Having pioneered a technique a few years earlier for distilling a spirit that was unusually free of the unpleasant compounds generated during distillation (principally fusel oils), he marketed a clear spirit, Tiodubbelt Renadt Brännvin (Tenfold-Purified Spirit). To ease its passage on the drinks market, this was changed in time to Absolut Rent Brännvin – Absolutely Pure Spirit. The ~~me vodka was not used until the mid-twentieth century.

was demonstrably purer, and easier on the palate, than the clear spirit ᵤ being sold under the auspices of the state drink monopoly, and in the interest of proving the point, he laid on public ferry trips to the distillery on the island of Reimersholme, just outside Stockholm. Proceeds from his Absolutely Pure Spirit set Smith up for life, but a few years after his death in 1913 the Swedish state assumed a legal monopoly of all spirits production.

For many years, Smith's formula was sold under variations of the brand name he had given it. It was produced by a giant combine called the V&S (Vin & Sprit) Group, of which the ultimate proprietor was the Swedish government. V&S created the modern Absolut brand, with its eye-catching bottle design, in 1979, exactly a century after Smith had first formulated the product. In 2008, the brand was sold to the French international drinks group Pernod Ricard.

Since its relaunch, Absolut has been produced in Åhus in the region of Scania, in the deep south of the country. It is based on locally grown winter wheat. Distilled in column stills, the vodka is a blend of two spirits that have been subjected to slightly different distillation techniques, one resulting in a lower-strength spirit than the other, and with a little more character, giving the vodka its distinctive flavour. Absolut also eschews the use of sugar, which is a recourse of many other brands for textural purposes. For all that the name is Absolut, the final product isn't made in the style of certain ultra-rectified, ultra-purified Russian vodkas, and it doesn't go through the charcoal filtration accorded to many other brands. The water comes from the company's own deep well at Åhus, and also from melted ice from the river Torne in Jukkasjärvi.

The bottle is modelled on the pharmaceutical bottles of centuries gone by, a reminder that vodka was once recommended for medicinal purposes. To British consumers of a certain vintage, it looks like the bottles that their milk used to come in – with the addition of descriptive text and a cameo image on the bottle shoulder of its progenitor, Lars Olsson Smith.

Taste
The flagship blue label Absolut has a light, subtly aromatic nose, with hints of caramel. On the palate, it is invitingly herbal, malty, gently apothecarial, with insinuating spirity warmth and discreet backnotes of anise, caraway and celery seasoning. It can be drunk neat, but also makes a fine base for a whole range of mixers, from apple juice to tonic water.

A higher-strength version, Absolut 100, is bottled at 50% abv, and so mainly through retail outlets at airports. It is powerfully assertive on th and has subtle but distinct notes of the kinds of spices normally f akvavit or Swedish punsch. Caraway and cumin suggestions follow thro on the palate, and that complex of spicy, grainy notes helps to balance out the formidable alcohol hit, so that the finish is entirely warm and comforting rather than aggressive.

The flavoured versions offer a greengrocer's display of ripe fruits. All are bottled at 40% abv.

Citron is flavoured with extracts of lemon, lime, orange, mandarin and grapefruit – something for everyone. It is predominantly lemony on the nose, with finely pared zest predominating, and becomes sweeter and more grape-fruity on the palate.

Ruby Red is flavoured with pink grapefruit, the edgy sweet citrus note beautifully integrated into its spirity medium. The palate is almost spritzy with fresh grapefruit tones, with something of the light bitterness, even soapiness, of the peel, and leads to a very scented finish.

Mandrin uses mandarin and regular orange extracts in a vodka that smells brightly and sweetly of orange jelly. There is a definite flavour dimension of mandarin/tangerine on the palate, so that it tastes like a very boozy sorbet, with strong alcohol following up.

Raspberri has a rich, impressively ripe nose, with bags of pulpy, overripe raspberries picked off the bush at just the stage where they might smoosh between your fingers if you're not gentle enough with them. Delicate framboise-liqueur flavours dominate the rounded palate, and there is good fruit persistence on the finish.

Kurant, flavoured with natural extracts of blackcurrants, has a nicely pungent, cassis-like aroma, with the sharpness of freshly picked blackcurrants following on behind. The palate is intriguingly, and cleverly, balanced between ripe but restrained fruit and the grown-up punch of alcohol.

Apeach has a strong peachy nose with hints of yogurt and even tinned cling peaches, but is not in any way confected. There is an attractive balance of acid tang and juicy-ripe peach flesh on the palate, supported by warmth of spirit on the finish.

Pears is one of my favourites. It has a slight suggestion of peardrops, soon overlaid on the palate with the acidity of green Conference pears. The edginess of pear-skin continues through the vodka to a long, aromatic finish.

Mango, launched in 2008, combines the juiciness and slight powderiness of mango flesh with underlying notes of orange.

Made from	Winter wheat, spring water, river meltwater
ABV	40%
Proof	80
Website	www.absolut.com
Origin	Sweden

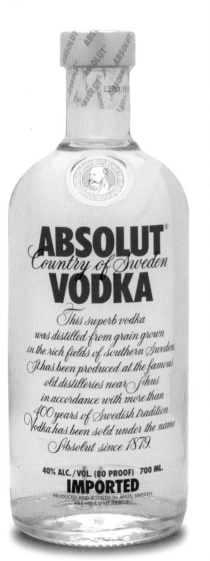

With **Peppar**, we leave the fruit-bowl behind, and venture into spicier territory. This is made with oils from bell peppers and red-hot jalapeño chillies, as well as admixtures of green tomato and herbs. The initial aromatic notes of chopped green pepper are followed by a dusting of black peppercorns, but the predominant note on the palate is vegetal, almost like chopped cabbage, seasoned with masses of black pepper. A must for a Bloody Mary or Bullshot.

Vanilia has masses of vanilla pod on the nose, with a sweet, creamy texture on the palate, a little like milk that has had whole vanilla infused in it. It finishes with gently spicy hints, and well-integrated spirit.

AKVINTA

The Mediterranean world is only just getting in on the vodka act. We hardly associate the spirit of the frosty north with the sun-splashed lands of southern Europe, and yet here too, exciting things are happening. Croatia's Akvinta is a leading player in the premium stakes in this part of the world.

Croatia lies on the eastern side of the Adriatic, facing Italy. The production of Akvinta takes place in one of the last great unravaged landscapes of southern Europe, a karst valley about 50 km (30 miles) from the coast.

The country boasts the third largest reserves of fresh water on the continent, and it is crystal-clear spring water from the mountains that goes into this vodka. The purity of the sea breezes is held to ensure that the spirit absorbs no trace elements from the atmosphere.

Its base is wheat grown organically in the northern Italian region of Emilia-Romagna, which the producers consider to be of more reliable quality than northern European grain because of the longer exposure to the sun it receives during the growing season. Akvinta employs an elaborate system of five separate filtrations for the water, each filtering element being more luxurious than its predecessor. Birch charcoal is the traditional enough starter, but this is then followed by marble, silver, gold and platinum, the last adding, we are told, unexpected subtleties to the aftertaste. Having gone through this expensive finishing school, the water is thought suitably refined to mix with the spirit, and then the whole blend is filtered once more.

British designers were responsible for the head-turning bottle, on which the brand name is written vertically in a stylish cursive script, while the base of the bottle is shaded red to match the capsule.

Taste
The nose of Akvinta is as pure as those multiple filtrations lead us to expect. It has the antiseptic tang of a clean Russian-style vodka. On the palate, it is weighty, serious stuff, perfectly streamlined in its contours, and the finish does indeed have discreet, complex notes of gentle spice such as caraway.

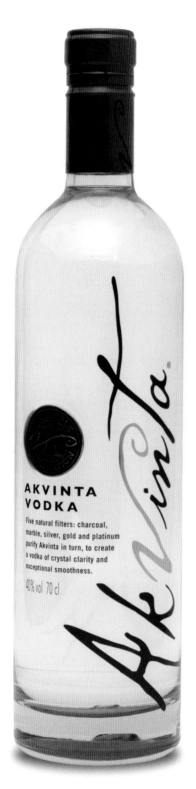

Made from	Italian wheat, Croatian mountain spring water
ABV	40%
Proof	80
Website	www.akvinta.com
Origin	Croatia

It makes a fine shot served with ice and a twist of lemon peel, but if you're going to mix it, I'd be inclined to treat it gently, perhaps with a little freshly juiced orange for a very grown-up Screwdriver.

BALKAN

Because the distillation of vodka eventually produces a spirit of nearly 100% alcohol, there has always been a subculture – both official and unofficial – in its homelands of taking it in stronger form than the average product. The Polish Pure Spirit bottled at 96% abv, which was so dear to my own student generation, was an obvious example, and here is another.

Balkan was launched in the UK in 2002. Made in Bulgaria, it is a grain vodka that has only been diluted down to 88%. It has been triple-distilled for smoothness of texture, and is not in any way to be confused with a bulk-produced industrial product. It is in fact made in small batches like many of the premium vodkas in this book, and the label comes adorned in its export markets with an extensive array of cautionary health messages. You have been warned.

The packaging, somehow fittingly, makes the product look like something you might find in a pharmacy, with its forbidding black lettering. The strength is shown in both the proof and percentage systems, and the brand name is printed in the Cyrillic alphabet used in Russia, Bulgaria and the Balkan countries.

Taste
Balkan should be served directly from the deepfreeze, but it absolutely must be mixed or diluted. In the course of my researches, dear reader, I was silly enough to taste it neat, and my palate didn't forgive me for many minutes. On the nose, it is naturally full of intimidating spirit strength, but balanced by rounded grainy notes. It is impossible to hold in the mouth without some admixture, but blended with freshly squeezed fruit juices or plenty of tonic water, some of its power can be tamed.

Its advertising lines are 'To be kept behind bars', and 'Not for everyone', in recognition of its terrifying potency, and the drink is sold with various recommendations for its consumption, such as 'A maximum of two measures per person' for those over 21. It's a fascinating product, but one that finally leaves you feeling glad that not all alcohol is as challenging as this.

Made from	Grain, and a dash of water
ABV	88%
Proof	176
Website	www.wineandspirit.com/balkan176.htm
Origin	Bulgaria

БАЛКАН®

BALKAN 176° VODKA

SUPER STRENGTH TRIPLE - DISTILLED
DELUXE GRAIN VODKA

70 cl ℮   IMPORTED FROM THE BALKANS
          HANDLE WITH GREAT CARE

88% vol
(176° US proof)

BELVEDERE

An established upmarket brand, Belvedere once had a lot more elbow room in the luxury vodka market than today's considerably more crowded scene allows for. It is named after the landmark Belweder Palace in Warsaw, once the home of Polish royalty, later the seat of government, and now reserved for visiting dignitaries and ceremonial state occasions.

The vodka is produced by Polmos Zyrardów in the Mazowsze (Mazovia) region of eastern Poland. It is made exclusively from rye, specifically a Polish variety known as Dankowski Gold, and distilled four times in copper column stills. Water from artesian wells is blended with the distillate, and then three separate filtrations are carried out to ensure crystalline purity.

In addition to the plain vodka, there are two flavour variants, developed by consultant Elie-Arnaud Denoix. Based on pure fruit macerations, these are Pomarańcza (a blend of different orange varieties with a touch of lime) and Cytrus (lemon, also with a seasoning touch of lime).

Belvedere derives from an Italian phrase meaning 'beautiful to see', the equivalent of the French *belle vue*. The design of the bottle captures the spirit of both the phrase and the palace, an image of which is printed on the back of the bottle, so that it appears in majestic, magnified clarity when viewed from the front. The current building dates from the early nineteenth century, its neoclassical porticoed entrance framed by winter trees in the bottle image.

Taste
The neutral Belvedere is almost unscented, and uncoils itself sinuously on the palate, with very gentle flavours for a rye vodka. The spirit is velvet-soft and caramelly, leading to warmer herb tones on the finish.

In 2008, Belvedere launched a high-strength version, Intense, packaged in a sultry black bottle at a sultry 50% abv.

Made from	Rye, artesian mineral water
ABV	40%
Proof	80
Website	www.belvedere-vodka.com
Origin	Poland

Pomarańcza has jellyish orange fruit on the nose, with a touch of orange blossom, good citric fullness in the mouth, a convincing real fruit flavour, and pleasantly balanced alcohol.

Cytrus has a definite mixed lemon-and-lime nose, a marmaladey palate, but with much less abrasively obvious fruit than some other lemon vodkas. The finish is hottish but manageable, making it a natural hit in a blend with freshly squeezed orange juice. Both of these products go cloudy with extreme chilling and mixing, a reaction to the essential oils they contain.

BLAVOD

The founder of London's Blavod company, Mark Dorman, hit upon the idea for the drink during an idle moment in a bar in San Francisco. Ordering a vodka, he was presented with a potentially bewildering range of 28 different brands, whereas a much starker and simpler option was offered when he ordered a coffee. Black or white? What if the same straightforward choice was offered to vodka drinkers?

For those who had always dreamed of being able to take their vodka black, Blavod came to the rescue in 1998. It is not quite black so much as indigo, or at least the bluish-black of the ink with which older readers may once have filled their fountain pens. Despite its awe-inspiring hue, Blavod is a neutral vodka in terms of its taste.

The colour is derived from catechu, the extract of a species of acacia tree native to southern and eastern Asia and the Indian Ocean area, produced by boiling the wood and then evaporating the brew to recover a glossy, semi-solid residue high in tannins. It is used in dyeing and tanning, as well as in ayurvedic medicine as an astringent and breath-freshener, and to staunch nosebleeds. Blavod's catechu is sourced from a Burmese strain of the tree.

Lest we imagine that this is a mere novelty product, it is worth noting that one of its earliest backers was no less august a personage than Baron Eric de Rothschild, head of Bordeaux's Château Lafite, who is reported to have invested around £2 million ($3 million) in the drink.

The clear bottle allows you to appreciate the Hammer Horror colour of the vodka, the effect of which is dramatically accentuated by unsubtle blood-red lettering. On its own in a glass, it looks vaguely alarming, with its blue-black, chemistry-set colour.

Blavod floats are popular among the cocktail set. If you fill a glass with ice, add a mixer, then slowly pour in the spirit, it will hover over the top of the drink like a lowering thundercloud. A Black Bull consists of ice, Red Bull and Blavod in that order.

Made from	Molasses, black catechu
ABV	40%
Proof	80
Website	www.blavod.com
Origin	UK (England)

Taste

The nose is pretty neutral, with perhaps the faintest suggestion of berries, and its quick, clean impact on the palate ensures it doesn't hang around with any aftertaste, other than a moderate spirit punch. It will also leave you with a most attractive blue tongue.

BORU

This Irish vodka aims for purity in taste and purism in its approach. It sets out specifically to be a vodka for drinking straight, in the Slavic style, with ice and perhaps no more than a lemon twist to show at its best. Its name commemorates the tribal king, Brian Boru, who united the Irish people under his reign in the early years of the eleventh century, and died seeing off the Vikings heroically at the Battle of Clontarf in 1014.

Produced at the Carbery distillery in County Cork, the vodka is subjected to five distillations and is filtered through oak charcoal (around 3 m/10 feet of it) in the traditional manner for extra smoothness. In recent years, it has made significant inroads into the US market, and the original neutral style has been joined by Orange, Citrus (lemon) and Crazzberry (cranberry and raspberry) variants.

There is certainly enough softness and cleanness in the plain version to make this vodka a winner when served neat. What you are looking for when you drink a vodka without accompaniments is a round, mellow mouth-feel without the aggressive edge of a cheaper spirit, and Boru undoubtedly delivers on that front.

The bottle design is as sleek and clean as the spirit itself, with the sword and shield of Brian Boru forming a motif above the brand name. It reflects the fact that this brand is intended to appeal to a more mature and discerning constituency than those products that are targeted at the younger 'lifestyle' market.

Taste
There is a distinct sweetness to the nose of the flagship bottling, with notes of caramel, even vanilla, coming through, supported by something luxurious like soft new leather. On the palate, it's supple and contoured, with a firm but mellow spirit hit, leading to a gentle, caramelly finish.

Of the flavoured versions, the **Crazzberry** is the standout, with luscious raspberry-ripple ice-cream scents and a decent red berry palate, with that

Made from	Barley, Irish spring water
ABV	37.5%
Proof	75
Website	www.boru.com
Origin	Ireland

creaminess in the fruit proving very appealing. It would be excellent in a cream-based cocktail. I find the flavour of the **Citrus** a little shy. It hasn't the upstanding tang of other lemon vodkas.

BRECON FIVE

A product of the Penderyn distillery in the mountainous Brecon Beacons national park in south-east Wales, Brecon Five has a ready-made niche for itself as the pre-eminent (indeed the only) Welsh vodka. What Penderyn lacks in size – and it is one of the smallest distilleries in the world – it makes up for in industrious versatility. It is also the source of a range of award-winning single malt whiskies, a gin and a cream liqueur called Merlyn.

Like its gin, Penderyn's vodka was launched in 2006. Humour was used in an attempt to position it in an already crowded market, but an advertising campaign playing on it being as unexpected as a Welsh women's quiz team knowing what the philosopher Kierkegaard was famous for upset the sensibilities of some.

The base grain spirit is produced by means of a five-column distillation, and then blended in small batches with a pot-still barley spirit and spring water. Drawn from the ground beneath the distillery, the water is naturally filtered through 340-million-year-old bedrock. The name reflects the five distillations the spirit undergoes.

When the last great ice age ended around 10,000 years ago, the ice sheets that covered northern Europe extended from the Arctic Circle as far as south Wales, a spot the Penderyn distillery now inhabits. This landmark location is acknowledged in the bottle's logo, which shows a capering ice man brandishing a couple of icicles against a frosted background. Ridges of ice taper away toward the neck, leaving the top part of the bottle crystal-clear, an expensive but undeniably effective bit of packaging.

Taste

There is an invigorating freshness to the nose and a dazzling purity as transparent as cellophane wrapping. On the palate, Brecon Five has a nice balance of savoury grain notes on a backdrop of sweet spirit, to make a powerful but well-composed vodka with a strong, high-octane finish. To me, this is a great vodka for mixing with fruit juices such as cranberry or grapefruit.

Made from	Wheat and barley, spring water
ABV	40%
Proof	80
Website	www.welsh-whisky.co.uk
Origin	UK (Wales)

CAPE NORTH

Sweden's Cape North – like many of the eastern European vodkas – is a spirit with royal connections. The company is based at Loviselund Manor, near the royal palace of Drottningholm on the island of Lovön, an address that traditionally supplied the royal family with premium vodka in the nineteenth century. The manor house had been a gift to King Gustav III (1746–1792) from his Queen Louisa.

It is in some senses a brand with dual nationality: while the company is Swedish, and the water that goes into the vodka is the internationally renowned pure spring water of Porla, the grain used is golden wheat grown in the Burgundy wine region of eastern France, and the production is carried out in Burgundy by a French master distiller, Jean Battault. This cross-cultural fusion harks back to the late eighteenth century, when King Gustav III was instrumental in opening court life to the cultural influence of France.

The company is owned by the Davidsson family, who have several generations' worth of experience in spirit production, while the distillation itself is contracted to a Burgundian house, Gabriel Boudier, established in 1874. In keeping with the jet-set lifestyle the brand promotes, it sponsors an annual series of powerboat rallies in Sweden and other European locations.

Cape North is distilled five times in small copper pot stills at the kind of sedate pace normally accorded to a cask-aged dark spirit, and is then passed through terracotta filters. The water is naturally filtered through 10,000-year-old layers of sedimentary rock and sand, making it among the purest in the world.

Great pains have been taken over the bottle design. It comes with a brushed aluminium screw cap with a specially designed seal to retain freshness, and the glass itself, especially the bottom, is thick enough to keep the contents at a chilly temperature for as long as possible once it is out of the freezer. The image is of a bracing Nordic winter scene of ice-blue skies and snow-shrouded mountain tops.

Made from	French wheat, Swedish spring water
ABV	40%
Proof	80
Website	www.capenorth.se
Origin	Sweden

Taste

I found gentle hints of caraway on the nose, very faintly suggestive of good Swedish akvavit, while the palate is impeccably rounded and silky in texture. There is a fleeting hint of something spicily aromatic (almost coffee) on the mid-palate, and the finish is firmly spirity but soft and sinuous too.

CARIEL

Some of the best premium vodkas on the market are emerging from Sweden. The trail blazed by Absolut has provided the impetus for a whole new generation of quality Swedish products, and the diversity of styles is breathtaking.

Cariel is a super-premium spirit that begins as a blend of two grain distillates, one from barley and one from winter wheat, both grown in Sweden. Micro-production is the only way to achieve a distinguished spirit, and this one is blended in small batches to ensure its distinctive character. When the balance of spirits is right, pure spring water is added to finish it.

Oddly, Cariel's bottling of neutral vodka followed its principal flavour variant on to the market. Cariel Vanilla had already established a reputation for itself as an ingredient in smart cocktail bars before the neutral version followed on suavely behind.

The four-sided bottle is a masterpiece of classic understatement, with the name and country printed directly on to the glass.

Taste

'Understated' is not the word one reaches for on tasting the neutral Cariel. It has an astonishingly fruity nose, even more so than its riotously fruity compatriot, Svensk (see page 188). There is a distinct sweet aroma of fresh pineapple, which opens out on the palate with pink grapefruit too. The alcohol is fairly gentle; what edge there is only helps to support and emphasize that exhilarating feeling of freshness and ripeness. A very attractive vodka.

It is a natural for blending in fruity cocktails, or just with a slug of fresh apple or pineapple juice. I'd even contemplate substituting it for plain white rum in certain cocktail recipes. Try it in an equal-measures mix with Cointreau and grapefruit juice for a bracing, first-drink-of-the-evening cocktail.

The **Vanilla**, bottled at 37.5% abv, is flavoured with pure vanilla extract, and has an intriguing flowery, nutty character. It makes a fine White Russian mixed with coffee liqueur and cream.

Made from	Wheat and barley, spring water
ABV	40.7%
Proof	81.4
Website	www.carielvodka.com
Origin	Sweden

CHARODEI

Distilled by a company that rejoices in the name of the Kryshtal Minsk Amalgamation Factory in the Belarussian capital of Minsk, Charodei makes a virtue of the fact that the production process doesn't involve a charcoal filtration. Instead, it relies for its smoothness on a technology that the producer has formulated and patented, in which the water used in its manufacture undergoes a primary purification. The lack of charcoal filtration, it is claimed, leaves some of the natural flavours of distillation in the finished product, rather than the antiseptically pure neutrality aimed at by so many other brands.

The name commemorates a national hero, just as Ireland's Boru (see page 68) and others do. Prince Vseslav, known as Charodei (the Sorcerer), became the unifier and first ruler of the Belarussian (White Russian) people from his power base in the principality of Polotsk in the feudal eleventh century. According to legend, the prince possessed magical powers and premonitory vision because he had been born with his mother's placenta stuck to his head. His reign was a long and generally benevolent one, lasting from 1044 to 1101. Even his death, just before Easter, was held to be mystically linked to the period of Christ's crucifixion and resurrection.

Kryshtal is the oldest vodka distiller in Belarus, having begun production in 1893. As well as the basic brand, a pair of super-premium bottlings, Lux and Super Lux, is available, made from a mixture of rye and wheat with artesian spring water and subjected to a quadruple distillation. Meanwhile, the original Vseslav version has won a trophy cabinet's worth of medals at international spirits competitions in the United States and Europe.

The frosted bottle goes for an ultra-traditional design that evokes the medieval past, with the princely ruler shown flanked by an honour guard of warlike female attendants.

Taste

On the nose, Vseslav Charodei is powerfully spirity, with a topnote of spearmint. Its texture in the mouth is weighty and oily, indicating that this is

Made from	Wheat, purified water
ABV	40%
Proof	80
Origin	Belarus

a serious spirit for drinking neat. There are gentle hints of aniseed in the flavour and an enticing, sweetish character to the alcohol, leading to a warm, sinuous, but interestingly edgy finish.

CHASE

He may look like one of the Chelsea set in his designer jeans, but Will Chase is a yeoman farmer in the best English idiom. He grows potatoes on what was once his father's farm, Rosemaund in Herefordshire, and tends a herd of dairy cows, to whom he talks solicitously every morning. He is the brains behind one of the UK's most successful gourmet potato chip brands of recent years, Tyrrells Crisps.

Will Chase is also a vodka enthusiast of long standing, and the move he made in 2008 into using some of his home-grown potatoes as the base for a distilled spirit felt to him a perfectly natural one, even though it is surely unprecedented in the world of niche food and drink.

The vodka is produced by artisan methods in a copper pot still at Rosemaund. It uses a blend of traditional potato varieties such as Golden Wonder, St Claire and Rosetta, and only those individual specimens that are too small to be turned into crisps go into the distillation. Small-batch production is the order of the day.

Launched with its final branding in the summer of 2008, Chase comes in a square-shouldered bottle with the brand name written vertically in an elegant black cursive script. Where other potato vodkas have tended to be modest about their principal ingredient, Chase makes a proud selling-point of it, announcing itself as 'English Potato Vodka'.

Taste
The vodka has a bright, slightly fruity nose, and a delightfully fresh, creamy palate with a hint of toffeeish sweetness. There is a toastiness hovering somewhere too, as though the flavour is gesturing toward sautéed potatoes as well as buttery mash, and that vigorous freshness recurs on the finish, where the alcohol is nicely integrated into the overall composition of the drink.

For me, this would make a good, assertive base for a spicy Bloody Mary, and it is also a winner in that much-underrated combination, vodka and apple juice.

Made from	Potatoes
ABV	40%
Proof	80
Website	www.williamschasedistillery.com
Origin	UK (England)

CHEKOV IMPERIAL

Chekov Imperial is a proprietary vodka brand of the large UK cash-and-carry company, Booker, original sponsors of the famous literary prize for fiction. It is sold from retail and catering outlets within the UK, and has proved popular at the value-conscious end of the market.

The product is bottled at two strengths, a Red Cap version at 37.5% abv and the significantly stronger Blue Cap at 45.5%. Both vodkas are triple-distilled for smoothness, but are very much aimed at the mixed-drinks and cocktails set, rather than the reflective, neat-sipping aficionado. That said, they are not without their own character.

The label design references Russian style, as befits a vodka named after the great Russian dramatist, Anton Chekhov, and is not dissimilar to that sported by the international brand leader, Smirnoff.

Taste
A strongish spirit hit is in evidence on the nose of the **Red Cap**, but in a warm and caramelly rather than abrasive vein, while the palate is spice-tinged with hints of fennel and caraway seeds, leading to a long, fairly complex finish.

The **Blue Cap** is intriguingly different, with a slight sour-cream aroma, even a bit of vanilla, and then a distinctly sweet, creamy, toffeeish palate, supported by a burly, assertive alcohol presence. This is the kind of vodka to use in a Black Russian, mixed with Tia Maria or other dark coffee liqueur, with cola to taste.

Made from	Grain
ABV	37.5%
Proof	75
Origin	UK (England)

CHOPIN

A Polish vodka named after one of the country's most famous sons is bound to have a lot going for it among a discerning, cultured audience. The Ministry of Culture in Poland took a little persuading to approve the brand name initially, but the Polmos Siedlce distillers prevailed, and this premium potato vodka has been associated with the composer since its launch in 1993.

It isn't just the production process that makes Chopin worthy of the description 'premium'. The potatoes that go into it are grown organically in one of the most fertile agricultural regions of the country, Podlasie in north-eastern Poland. Once an exotic luxury (when they first appeared on sale in Krakow in the mid-eighteenth century, they were more expensive than chocolate), potatoes are now a staple of the Polish diet. In the Podlasie region, they turn up on the menu in the form of *kartacze*, meat and potato dumplings, or *babka*, a 'pie' of baked shredded potato bound with egg and pork fat.

The potato used in Chopin is a high-starch variety named Stobrawa, with around 3 kg (7 pounds) of potatoes needed for each bottle. Distilled at a state-of-the-art facility in Krzesk, the vodka undergoes four distillations, which the producers reckon is the optimum number for a potato vodka. Such is the commitment to quality, Polmos Siedlce assures us that if a sample of the vodka is found to contain the smallest imbalance in the flavour, that entire batch will be discarded.

A distinguished frosted glass bottle features a cameo image of Frédéric Chopin imprinted on the back of the bottle, which becomes enlarged when viewed through the spirit.

Taste
There is a definite potato suggestion to the aroma in the glass, allied to strong, pure spirit. On the palate, the vodka is assertive in character, with pronounced edges and a note like boiled waxy potatoes. The finish is powerful and long, making this a good vodka for mixing with other forthright flavours, such as freshly squeezed lime juice and sugar syrup, or a dash of single malt whisky for an unforgettable Smoky Martini.

Made from	Potatoes, spring water
ABV	40%
Proof	80
Website	www.chopinvodka.com
Origin	Poland

CIROC

What raw material do we expect vodka to be made from? A cereal grain, or blend of grains? Or potatoes? Try grapes. Cîroc is the world's first vodka to be made from wine grapes and, as such, it just had to come from France. Fermented as for wine, and then distilled into a neutral, clear, rectified spirit, the drink conforms to the European Union's legal definition for vodka, and thus it is proudly labelled. It is the only vodka in this book to be the combined work of a vineyard manager and a master distiller.

The grapes used in Cîroc are a pair of white varieties: principally Mauzac, a speciality of the Gaillac region in south-west France, along with Ugni Blanc, which is more usually distilled to make cognac. The grapes are left on the vine to attain maximum ripeness, and then hand-picked. Mauzac makes a crisp, herbaceous style of dry white wine, not unlike a Sauvignon Blanc, so how does it fare in a clear spirit?

Macerated on the grapeskins to enhance complexity, and subjected to a cool fermentation to preserve fruit character, Cîroc really does start out as a wine. It is distilled five times (the last time in a specially designed copper pot still) to remove impurities and acquire the clean, fresh taste of a premium vodka.

A TV advertising campaign for Cîroc in 2008 saw the brand being aimed directly at a young, cocktail-crazy audience. In the middle of the goings-on at a frenetic nightclub, the rap star Diddy is an oasis of cool, seated at a table while he is served a succession of Cîroc cocktails.

The bottle is almost as cool as Diddy himself. It's a tall cylinder with square shoulders, and an inset blue disc that is the brand's logo. A blue-shaded base adds to the aura of icy purity.

Taste
Not surprisingly, Cîroc has an obvious grapy nose. It's intensely fruity in aroma, with notes of orange and lemon preceding the uprush of spirit. The attack on the palate is also sweetly fruity and grapy, so that if it were a wine, it might be something like a dry Muscat (although there are no Muscat

Made from	Wine grapes
ABV	40%
Proof	80
Website	www.cirocvodka.com
Origin	France

grapes in it). It's hard to decide whether it will catch on in any big way, but this is an interesting product. As its producer suggests, it makes a great ingredient in fruity cocktails such as Cosmopolitans and Sea Breezes.

COLD RIVER

Outside Poland, potato vodkas are a minority pursuit. Britain's Chase vodka (see page 68) is one western European pioneer, but there is still a feeling among consumers that quality vodka ought to be made from grain. Here is another brand that sets out to demonstrate that it ain't necessarily so.

Cold River is very much a twenty-first-century conception. It was the creation of brothers Lee and Donnie Thibodeau, scions of a potato-farming family in the New England state of Maine. In these days of regional gastronomic specialities, Maine has developed quite a reputation for its potatoes, and the Thibodeaus' farm is plumb in the middle of the premier growing district.

All aspects of production are overseen by the distiller Chris Dowe, from the planting of potato seeds to the bottling of the finished vodka. This is an operation very much in tune with natural cycles, centring on the eponymous Cold River that runs down the western side of the state of Maine. Its waters nourish the potato fields, and the aquifer that it flows into provides the water with which the vodka is blended.

The broad, majestic sweep of the river is depicted on the glass of the square-shouldered bottle, which incorporates some handwritten script as well as block lettering, to lend the product something of the artisanal feel with which the whole enterprise began.

Taste
Cold River has an obvious potato bouquet, both waxy and buttery, with the suggestion of mashed potato made with plenty of butter and milk. The palate is richly rounded and soft, displaying evidence of careful filtration, but still showing the fluffy potato character of the nose. It finishes with the gentle heat of its spirit, more as a discreet reminder than a forthright announcement.

The Thibodeaus suggest shaking it with ice and a splash of amaretto or Drambuie, and indeed those richer spirits flavoured with almonds or honey

Made from	Potatoes, river aquifer water
ABV	40%
Proof	80
Website	www.coldrivervodka.com
Origin	United States

are happier marriages to me than anything overtly fruity. That said, it also mingles well with cider.

Cold River's first flavour variant, using Maine's other great sought-after crop, **wild blueberries**, was launched in 2008.

CRISTALNAYA

While Cristalnaya may sound like a Russian product, it is in fact more of a homage to the Russian tradition, and is produced in the UK by the long-established brewing and distilling company G & J Greenall. The company was founded in Warrington, Cheshire, in 1761 by Thomas Dakin, in the wake of what one might politely call the 'gin craze' in England. His mission was to produce a better-quality gin than most of the poorer people had access to, and his target market included wealthy foreign travellers passing through town on the journey north. Greenall still produces over 70% of the own-brand gin and vodka sold in the UK, supplying to all the major supermarket chains.

Cristalnaya is made explicitly in the Russian style, with particular emphasis on the techniques established by the celebrated scientist, Dmitri Mendeleev during the reign of Tsar Alexander III. Conceived under the auspices of Britain's only woman master distiller, Joanne Simcock, Cristalnaya is a triple-distilled grain vodka that also contains a bouquet of natural botanical ingredients that remain a trade secret. 'A liquid as pure as diamonds' is the declared aim, and the vodka is bottled at the optimum vodka strength determined by Mendeleev's researches, 38% abv. (The bottling strength of 40% in many traditional vodkas derived from a rounding-up back in the nineteenth century, in order to simplify the tax calculation, which was based on alcoholic degree.)

Cristalnaya comes in a modern, handsome, broad-shouldered bottle; the blue label is near the shoulder and discreetly narrow, showing the vodka to its best advantage.

Taste
It has a fairly light wheaty nose, very simple, straightforward and clean in the Russian manner, and a sinuous, obviously refined palate marked by some gentle sweetness. There is an edge to the spirit, but it isn't at all obtrusive, and the vodka finishes with suggestions of a distant, well-judged herbal lift (from those botanicals, presumably).

Made from	Wheat, botanicals
ABV	38%
Proof	76
Website	www.cristalnaya.com
Origin	UK (England)

As well as using it in classic recipes like vodka martini and Bloody Mary, Cristalnaya also propose Cristal Sparkler, a mix of two parts Cristalnaya to three parts champagne, served well chilled in a flute glass.

CYTRYNOWKA

Long before all the modern citrus and lemon vodka variants, the spirit producers of Poland and Russia had developed aromatized versions of their basic grain spirits. The initial impulse for these various flavouring elements may well have been to disguise the rank nature of rough-and-ready distillates, often pungent with compounds such as aldehydes and fusel oil.

A herbalist's storecupboard of roots, leaves and berries was pressed into service, and so in time were fruits and fruit extracts. Since nothing succeeds quite like strong liquor full of the exuberant natural flavours of ripe fruits, these became legitimate styles of vodka in their own right, dry spirits for sipping neat, with or after food.

There are records of lemons being used to flavour Polish vodka as far back as the sixteenth century. That may come as a surprise, but we know that oranges and lemons were being imported from southern Europe at least as early as the fifteenth century. They were generally pickled in salt (indeed were sometimes imported already in this state), or preserved by macerating in sugar syrup. Even in modern times, citrus fruits retained the aura of a luxury festive food item. In the early 1970s, the communist authorities bought off one of the periodic bouts of labour unrest in Poland by distributing shiploads of imported lemons and oranges for a morale-boosting Christmas feast.

Russia had its *limonnaya*, and Poland created *cytrynówka*. These spirits were made by steeping the skins of the fruit in the vodka. These days, the process is altogether more refined. The spirits are still flavoured by maceration of the peels, but the fruit doesn't have to undergo preservation first. This results in a drink that genuinely smells and tastes of lemons fresh off the tree. Polmos Józefów makes this Cytrynówka by macerating both the lemon skins and some of the freshly harvested leaves of the lemon tree.

Taste
What you see in the glass is a luminous yellow spirit, but the lemon scents are relatively restrained. There is a faintly dessert-like quality to the flavour, as of lemon meringue pie or lemon tart, although the drink itself isn't sweet. What

Made from	Grain, lemon peel, lemon leaves
ABV	40%
Proof	80
Origin	Poland

I particularly like about it is that it has more balanced alcohol than most of the modern flavoured vodkas, because it is based on good, carefully distilled grain spirit. And it follows up those lemon dessert flavours with a pleasing bitter twist at the end.

Cytrynówka is just asking to be paired with freshly squeezed orange juice (blood orange is great) and plenty of ice, for a much more interesting V&O than the one you are used to drinking.

DANNOFF

Part of the global UB drinks company based in Sheffield in the UK, Dannoff is a Latvian vodka that aims for something like premium quality at something less than a premium price. At present, there are surprisingly few vodkas in evidence on the export markets from the Baltic states of Latvia, Lithuania and Estonia, so Dannoff has a chance to make a name for itself.

It began its international career with a launch into the UK off-trade in September 2008, from which it is expected to take the rest of Europe by storm. Produced in the Latvian capital, Riga, it is a stablemate of the national speciality, Latvijas Balzams, a dark brown bitter digestif traditionally added to coffee.

Dannoff is made from winter wheat and undergoes four distillations to ensure maximum purity and neutrality. It is then blended with demineralized spring water that has been through a softening treatment, and the resulting mix is filtered through activated charcoal to remove any remaining impurities. A virtue is made of the fact that no citrus-based additives are used in its manufacture, as is the case with many other neutral vodkas, thus maintaining the product in the dead neutral pH range – neither acid nor alkaline.

A fairly traditional bottle design features white and gold lettering and a discreet heraldic crest – nothing showy.

Taste
The nose suggests a lively spirit, clean and fresh but slightly prickly, too. It is gentler on the palate, its alcohol rounded to the extent of taking on a touch of caramel sweetness, even light toffee, reflecting the quadruple distillation. That leads on to a rounded, silky finish, announcing that this is indeed a classy product for the price.

This is a good vodka for mixing, although the palate is soft enough to allow the spirit to be drunk neat over ice. Its silkiness of texture makes it an excellent base for a vodka martini.

Made from	Wheat, spring water
ABV	37.5%
Proof	75
Website	www.dannoff.com
Origin	Latvia

DANZKA

Among the many comparatively new premium Scandinavian vodkas, Danzka is one of the more distinguished. Launched in 1989, it drew on the 150 years of distillation experience boasted by Danish Distillers of Copenhagen. In modern fashion, it presents both a neutral vodka and an impressive line-up of contemporary fruit flavours.

The red-label flagship bottling is made from home-grown Danish wheat and demineralized water. It is made by the continuous distillation method, in which the spirit runs uninterruptedly through a patented six-column apparatus, as opposed to being batch-produced in pot stills. Continuous distillation is often held to produce a more aromatic spirit than pot-still (the usual illustrative comparison is between armagnac and cognac respectively). That may not seem quite so important in the case of a plain vodka, but it truly does make a difference. Transfer through carbon and fine membrane filters completes the process.

Few vodkas have quite such distinctive presentation as Danzka, which comes in a handsome aluminium flask: the material was chosen because it chills down more quickly and is better at retaining ice-cold temperatures than glass. It feels like something you might expect to be opening on a camping holiday, but it certainly does the trick.

Taste
The plain vodka has an astonishingly citrus-fresh nose, leading into a light and appealing palate that seems hardly spirity at all, so beautifully softened is it, and there are notes of lemon pith and bitter citrus on the finish. It's the kind of vodka that effortlessly shines out in a line-up of neutral spirits, and is excellent for serving ice-cold and neat with perhaps just a spritz of lemon peel squeezed into it, to emphasize that citrus tang.

Among the flavoured bottlings, the slightly awkwardly named **Cranberyraz** stands out. Although Ireland's Boru (see page 58) produces a flavoured vodka based on this blend, Danzka's was the world's first. It has extravagantly creamy fruit on the nose, and a distinct impression of the lactic

Made from	Whole wheat, demineralized water
ABV	40%
Proof	80
Website	www.danzka.com
Origin	Denmark

richness of ice-cream flavours on the palate, with the 40% spirit bursting through on the finish. Try it in a three-parts-to-one mix in a glass of non-vintage champagne.

Danzka also produces **Citrus** (lemon), **Currant** (blackcurrant) and **Grapefruit** flavours.

DQ

Ultra-premium vodka hardly gets more exciting-looking than DQ. Is it a bottle of spirits, or is it a lava lamp? Its sleek elegance combines with formidable weight, the standard litre bottle and its incredibly heavy top demanding an effort of concentration in the handling that reflects the status of the contents. Nobody is going to be sloshing this thoughtlessly around at a student party.

Launched in 2009, the drink is the creation of the Nordic Spirit company, and represents a determination to return the Swedish vodka-making tradition to its roots, by presenting a pure, unmixed distillate that hasn't been adulterated along the way with cheaper spirits, as with the entry-level brands.

It is based on wheat planted during the autumn and left to brave the extremities of the northern winter, conditions that allow the cereal itself to survive but that kill off any biological impurities. Having already spent the winter months absorbing soil nutrients, the wheat then continues to develop during the extended hours of daylight in the summer, when the phenomenon of the midnight sun comes into its own.

Continuous distillation in multiple column stills creates a singularly pure spirit, which is then blended with untainted water from the Malmköping springs, to which the distillery has a direct pipeline. This part of south-east Sweden has been a site for spirits production since the early part of the nineteenth century, owing to the preternatural purity of the water. The final stage in the production is the back-blending of a little additional pure spirit, of a richer character than the original distillate, to round out and harmonize the flavours.

A design masterstroke inspired by nuclear engineering, the bottle is a tall, blue, straight-sided cylinder of Italian glass with a massively weighty screw-cap. Running down the centre is a shiny column of brushed aluminium, resembling a plutonium rod, through which the vodka travels when poured, being dispensed through a nozzle that allows a controlled amount of air to get into it. The process is theoretically analogous to allowing wine to breathe.

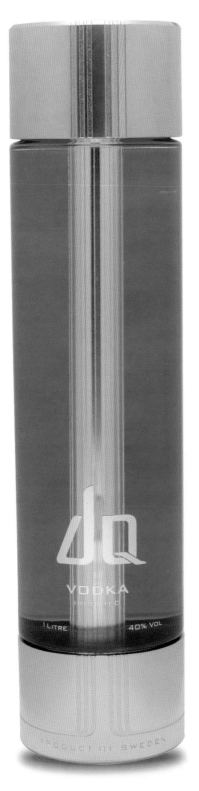

Made from	Wheat, spring water
ABV	40%
Proof	80
Website	www.dqvodka.com
Origin	Sweden

Despite appearances, the packaging is allegedly entirely carbon-neutral in its production.

Written along the back of the bottle is an inspirational quote from Albert Einstein: 'Imagination is everything. It is the preview of life's coming attractions.'

Taste

DQ (the initials stand for a Swedish phrase meaning 'distilled intelligence') has a very gentle, whisperingly shy nose that slowly releases notes of aniseed, fennel and liquorice. These combine on the palate in gorgeous array, all wrapped up in warming but supremely tactful alcohol, to make a hugely complex, thrilling vodka with a long, spice-toned finish. It is a grand product for drinking neat, and indeed hardly even requires much chilling, but also makes an incomparable vodka martini.

EFFEN

Effen was created with the contemporary style-bar phenomenon in mind; the recipe was developed by a panel of bartenders. It comes in a designery bottle with a pair of flavour extensions, which is what the modern cocktail crowd expects of today's vodka brands.

The name is a Dutch adjective meaning 'smooth', 'even' or 'balanced', which gives an admirably clear indication of the intentions of the distiller. It is made from wheat grown in northern Holland; wheat is favoured because it contains fewer fatty acids than other types of grain. Effen is produced by continuous distillation at lower temperatures than other vodkas, which minimizes the caramelization that can give a harder taste to a clear spirit.

Filtration is an intentionally topsy-turvy process, with the usual gravitational trickle through charcoal being rejected in favour of a rising filtration through densely packed peat. Both the choice of material and the direction of flow reduce the occurrence of 'channelling', whereby the vodka makes little tunnels for itself in the filtering medium, managing as it does so to hold on to some of its unwanted impurities.

The water used in the blending is purified by reverse osmosis, in which it is forced through a fine membrane at very high pressure. This emboldens its producer to announce on the bottle that the vodka is made with 'perfect water'.

The bottle is a masterpiece of ergonomic design. A sturdy cylinder, it is wrapped in a rubber sleeve that not only allows the bartender a better grip when it's wet with condensation, but also acts as insulation to keep the contents chilled for longer. Each sleeve is applied by hand: the inside is sprayed with deionized water, then it is slipped onto the bottle, in line with a small ridge, obviating the need for any kind of adhesive. And if that's not attention to detail, it's hard to know what is.

Taste
Effen has a bouquet of spritzy citric freshness, with a touch of mandarin coming through. It strikes the palate with a positive, bracing but rounded

Made from	Wheat, 'perfect water'
ABV	40%
Proof	80
Website	www.effen.com
Origin	Netherlands

impact, the orangey note gaining point from the soft spirit. The finish is warmish but gentle, weighty but graceful, in a vodka full of appealing balance.

The flavour variants, bottled at just below vodka strength (35%), aim for distinction by mixing natural fruit flavours with real vanilla extract. **Black Cherry** is full of the marzipan-like flavours of cherry-stones (not unlike a good cherry brandy) in a densely rich palate profile. The vanilla note is more subtle, but adds to a pleasant overall suggestion of cherry cheesecake. Try it in a spin on the traditionally gin-based Singapore Sling, with lemon juice, a touch of Cointreau and soda. **Raspberry** is equally appealing, with the aroma of rich raspberry ice-cream. It's more obviously enhanced by its vanilla than the Black Cherry, and is pleasantly soft, creamy and rounded on the palate. Try it with white grape or apple juice.

ERISTOFF

Welcome to Virshan, or the Land of the Wolf. Invading Persians gave the territory this name in the sixteenth century – a time when Georgia was cut off from the Russian motherland by incursions from the two predominant Muslim powers of the day, firstly the Ottoman Empire and then the Savafid dynasty of Iran – and the grey wolf has been Georgia's national symbol ever since.

The brand name of this vodka derives from the name taken by various feuding aristocratic families of the region, Eristavi. It meant 'leader of an army', and was thus a means of establishing martial credentials during a time of political turbulence. Many of the Eristavis were formidable warriors. It was a scion of the north-western branch of the Eristavis, Prince Ivan from the province of Racha, who helped formulate the recipe for this vodka in 1806. It is still in use today.

The last male descendant of the vodka Eristoffs, Prince Nicolai Alexandrovich, died in 1970. Although he had a sister, Olga, who outlived him by 21 years, it is Nicolai's name that appears on the label of every bottle of Eristoff vodka. The brand is now part of the Bacardi group.

A bell-bottomed bottle boasts an embossed crown above a dark blue label, with a legend in Cyrillic script around the base. This reads, 'Original Recipe of Prince Eristoff, 1806'. There is also a more modern logo, just beneath the label, of a wolf in silhouette performing the first duty of a wolf – howling at the moon.

Taste
Eristoff is triple-distilled and then charcoal-filtered. The result is a very clean vodka with a medicinally pure nose that contains a distant hint of lemon peel. The palate is dead neutral in the Russian style, but the spirit is pleasingly smooth and soft all the way through to the finish.

This is a fine vodka for drinking neat, or else for serving with plenty of ice and perhaps just a slice of lime, but no mixer. Otherwise, it works well with good lemonade and even, as its proprietor company suggests, with today's energy drinks.

Made from	Rye
ABV	37.5%
Proof	75
Website	www.eristoff.com
Origin	Georgia

EVOLUTION

This is one of those vodkas that has positioned Poland securely ahead of its eastern European neighbours when it comes to market innovation. There is only so much mileage to be had from the heritage route, from 200-year-old recipes and long-vanished aristocratic lineages. The future is now. Against that background, the name of this vodka is well chosen. It represents an organic, developmental approach to change in manufacture and marketing, while incorporating some of the best of the old ways into modern technology as discreetly as a blade of bison grass in a bottle of vodka. Evolution is the name of the game.

This is a rye vodka that uses the lauded Dankowski Gold grain, unblended with any other source material. It is handmade in small, controlled batches, and subjected to five separate distillations in pursuit of what the distiller terms a 'universal character'. It is then reduced with water that has been purified by high-pressure reverse osmosis.

The frosted bottle features runic symbols in Polish red and white, suggesting the elemental power of the sun.

Taste

The neutral vodka has a very discreet, clean nose with muted spirit impact, leading on to a soft, rounded palate, with some gentle lemony citrus influence, nicely integrated alcohol, and the richer finish of a rye vodka. It drinks well alone but mixes beautifully with lemonade, tonic or pressed apple juice.

Evolution **Bison Grass**, with its image of a grazing bison, is a traditionally made *zubrowka* style (see Zubrowka page 212). It has the customary delicate straw colour, as well as the immersed grass blade, the textbook grassy nose, backed by hints of camomile tea and woodruff, and a very gently sweet and hauntingly aromatic palate. It is less sharply perfumed than some, and rather the better for that. It's bottled at 40% abv. Mix with cloudy apple juice over ice, and garnish with a couple of apple wedges, for the classic Polish cocktail known as *szartlotka*.

Made from	Rye, purified water
ABV	37.5%
Proof	75
Website	www.dinsa.eu/ evolution.html
Origin	Poland

EXTRA ŻYTNIA

In 1999, this brand of vodka, made under contract with the original Polmos producer at Bielsko Biala in the deep south of Poland, was awarded its trademark after a painstaking comparative tasting of rye vodkas conducted by the Polish government. It was declared to be the most characteristic brand of rye vodka. This is a dry, thoroughly refined but intriguingly aromatic style of traditional Polish spirit.

The geographical lineage of many of the old Polish vodkas has become increasingly complicated in the modern era. Żytnia is the name of both a town and a lake in north-eastern Poland, although the distillery where Extra is now made is in the central Mazovia province.

It was announced by the Polish government in the summer of 2008 that it wanted to sell the Polmos Bielsko Biala distillery to a private investor, and we must hope that any future owner maintains the reputation and quality of this justly renowned product.

Highly purified neutral rye spirit is the basis of Extra Żytnia, which is blended with clear mountain water, then subjected to a multi-stage rectification process that ends with carbon filtering. A finely judged addition of aromatic fruit ingredients and a dash of apple spirit increase the drink's complexity. This is one of those vodkas that is on the cusp between one style and the other – neither strictly neutral, nor an out-and-out flavoured vodka.

The label shows a stalk of rye on a distinctively shaped waisted bottle known as a 'karat'.

Taste
There is a very faint golden tinge to the colour of Extra Żytnia, which has a sweetly rounded, rich rye nose and palate. The spirit is fairly assertive, but is sustained by a fascinating, caraway-scented, orchard fruit flavour (baking apples) that persists through to the long, dry finish.

Made from	Rye, mountain water, apple spirit
ABV	40%
Proof	80
Website	www.extrazytnia.com.pl
Origin	Poland

FINLANDIA

Like the United States, Finland underwent a prolonged period of alcohol prohibition, at almost exactly the same time, between 1919 and 1932. However, unlike in America, when the legislation was repealed, the state took over the monopoly of spirits production. Primalko, the national body, created Finlandia as an international brand in 1970, in an explicit attempt to rival the Russian vodkas from which Finland's vodka tradition had originally derived.

Proudly named after its homeland, Finlandia is made using Arctic spring water that is naturally filtered through a 10,000-year-old glacial moraine created in the last ice age. The grain that goes into it is the premium six-row strain of barley, so named for the six kernel rows in each head of the grain. Higher in protein, it is the sophisticated cousin of two-row barley, which is more suited to making beer.

Large swathes of Finland are relatively unmolested by agricultural intervention, and it is this pristine natural purity that Finlandia (and other Scandinavian vodkas) celebrates. The growing season is naturally very short, barley not being an especially hardy crop in cold conditions, but the saving climatic grace is the fabled phenomenon of the midnight sun that shines unceasingly through the summer months; it is acknowledged by being depicted on the Finlandia bottles.

The bottle design is minimally simple, with a little texturing in the clear glass to suggest a naturally formed hunk of Finnish glacier. In the case of the four flavoured versions, all labelled Fusion, the colours of the fruits are attractively reflected on the inside of the bottle's base.

Taste
Very clean on the nose, the neutral Finlandia has a bracingly pure palate with very discreet spirit. There is a distant hint of aniseed, but essentially it is the utterly uncomplicated purity of the spring water that shines through.

Made from	Six-row barley, glacial spring water
ABV	40%
Proof	80
Website	www.finlandia.com
Origin	Finland

Grapefruit has an acerbic yellow grapefruit nose, but is softer and gentler on the palate, with a suggestion of pineapple. The lovely **Lime** has pure zest and pared peel in the aroma, and a positively happy, zesty, alluring flavour. I found more of mandarin orange in the scent of the **Mango**, and a soft, jelly-like texture to the fruit in the mouth, while the **Cranberry** suggests raspberries and rosehips on the nose, and soft chewy sweets on the palate, rather than the bitterness of cranberries.

FLAGSHIP

Readers of the Cyrillic alphabet will note that the Russian name of this product is Flagman. The name is a homage to the founder and first admiral of the Russian naval fleet, Tsar Peter I, better known to history as Peter the Great. Having acceded to the throne in 1682 at the tender age of 10, Peter later studied navigation and the naval arts in the Netherlands in order to further his vision of turning imperial Russia into a maritime nation that could compete with the empires on its doorstep. The country's first naval base, at Taganrog on the Azov Sea, was opened in 1698.

Flagship is made at the Chernogolovka distillery near Moscow. A triple-distilled grain spirit, produced in strict accordance with the principles of Dmitri Mendeleev's distillation technique of 1894 (see Introduction, page 17), is blended with artesian water that has undergone a three-stage refinement process to soften it to the texture of water from mountain springs. Rectification under pressure is followed by a thorough filtration to achieve a palate-neutral Russian vodka.

Flagship enjoys the Russian equivalent of British 'By Appointment' status, counting the Kremlin among its customers. The embossed bottle boasts the emblem of the old Russian honorific Order of St Andrew the Apostle in a starburst motif around the label; the brand name appears in Cyrillic, with its western translation beneath.

Taste
The vodka has the clean, pungently antiseptic nose of a highly rectified spirit. As if in riposte to those who erroneously expect a neutral vodka to be light-bodied, the palate is weighty and authoritative, with evanescent notes of aniseed and fennel-seed coming through on the finish. This is big, powerful stuff, tasting perhaps slightly headier than 40%, but impeccably well-balanced anyway.

It makes a memorable neat shot, but also mixes well in the kinds of cocktails that don't attempt to disguise its inherent character too much. An unnamed Russian barman has come up with a successful mix with hazelnut-flavoured

Made from	Wheat, artesian spring water
ABV	40%
Proof	80
Website	www.flagshipvodka.co.uk
Origin	Russia

syrup and pineapple juice, and the company's website also lists a nice variation on the Moscow Mule formula, in which a tablespoonful of strawberry purée is added to the juice of a lime, a double-shot of Flagship and the traditional ginger ale top-up.

GINSENG VODKA

Made for the ominously named Functional Booze company of Sweden, Ginseng Vodka – or GV, as it prefers to be known – is no run-of-the-mill offering. It is made with pure mineral water, naturally filtered through sand and limestone, grain spirit, and of course ginseng, the plant remedy for which a welter of health claims has been made over the centuries.

A staple of Chinese herbal medicine, ginseng was described as 'calming the spirit and enlightening the mind' by the sixteenth-century herbalist, Li Shih-Chen. In modern times, it has been proposed by the alternative pharmacology industry as retarding the signs of aging, enhancing memory, stimulating the immune system and promoting male sexual vigour, any or all of which may be more speculative than proven claims.

Here, it appears in the context of a contemporary vodka packaged in a six-sided bottle, its name printed in bold vertical lettering on the inside, giving a multi-faceted, refracted effect.

Taste

There is a very distant note of something herbal on the nose; on the palate, a fairly straightforward neutral grain vodka is jollied up with a touch of herbal extract. It isn't enormously complex, but at least the spirit doesn't feel crude on the palate, and who knows? It might do you some good, taken in level-headed quantities.

One of the manufacturer's cocktail suggestions is a mix of three parts GV to two parts Midori (the Japanese melon liqueur) and one part blue curaçao, shaken with ice and served in a tall glass. The resulting concoction is a delicate spring green.

Made from	Wheat, ginseng, spring water
ABV	37.5%
Proof	75
Website	www.funbooze.com/gv.html
Origin	Sweden

GLEN'S

The second most important vodka brand in the UK in volume of sales, Glen's is a proprietary brand bottled at the Glen Catrine distillery in Ayrshire, Scotland. This operation is an offshoot of the Loch Lomond Distillery Co Ltd, a large-scale producer of Scotch whisky, gin and vodka, which itself began life as a small family firm with a single shop in Glasgow in the 1840s.

Glen's was originally known as Grant's vodka, until a legal ruling imposed a new name in 2003, to distinguish it from products made by William Grant & Sons. Its popularity in UK retail outlets has been undimmed by the rebranding and, at the time of writing, it is seriously challenging the leading white rum brand, Bacardi, in the league table of white spirit sales.

This is all the more remarkable given that the meteoric rise of Glen's in the market has been achieved without recourse to multi-million-pound advertising, pretentious labelling or lifestyle positioning. The brand is what it claims to be – an everyday spirit of reliable quality for the less extravagant end of the market.

The label sticks to the tried-and-true formula for proprietary vodkas, a red-and-white design that incorporates a heraldic logo.

Taste
I found a hint of juniper on the nose, which fleetingly suggests one of the less pungent brands of gin. The palate is rounded and soft, with gentle spirit warmth and a slight woody tone, derived from the use of sugar beet rather than grain. On the finish, there are subtle notes of spice: aniseed and coriander seeds.

Made from	Sugar beet
ABV	37.5%
Proof	75
Origin	UK (Scotland)

GORBATSCHOW

The German brand leader is named after the Russian who founded the company. Leontowitsch Gorbatschow, head of a successful distillery, fled St Petersburg with his family in the immediate aftermath of the October Revolution and settled in Berlin. There, he eventually resumed production, registering Gorbatschow as a German brand in 1921. These days, it is not only the best-selling vodka in Germany, but also the country's second largest spirit brand.

After the grain distillate is blended with soft water, Gorbatschow undergoes a painstaking triple charcoal filtration process at -12°C, resulting in a style of crystal purity that reflects its Russian origins.

It is bottled at a variety of strengths, with colour-coded labels: Blue (37.5%), Black (50%) and Red (60%). There is also a high-end product called Platinum 44, which receives several extra filtrations, and comes in a frosted bottle at the alcoholic potency indicated in its name. The appearance of a Citron variant suggests that the brand is about to make a debut in the flavoured sector.

With the exception of the Platinum 44, the Gorbatschow range is packaged in a distinctive bottle, the upper part of which recalls the onion domes of St Basil's Cathedral in Moscow.

Taste
The classic blue-label bottling offers a very discreet nose, not at all aggressive in its alcohol content, with just a touch of caramel wafer-biscuit lingering somewhere. The same note recurs on the palate, which is supported by gently softened spirit in a squeaky-clean Russian style, as befits its original provenance.

Gorbatschow is soft enough to drink just as it comes, but it is better as the basis for a mixed drink. Drink with orange or apple juice, or good still lemonade, without drowning it. The Platinum 44 should be drunk with nothing more than ice and a twist of lemon.

Made from	Grain, soft water
ABV	37.5%
Proof	75
Website	www.wodka-gorbatschow.de
Origin	Germany

GREEN MARK

Russian consumers might find it hard to believe, but the Green Mark brand is little known in the West. On its home turf this is the biggest brand of all, and indeed is one of the top five vodka brands in the world.

The name – Zelenaya Marka in Russian – refers to the seal of state approval that vodkas had to receive during the early years of the Soviet Union. After an initial flirtation with prohibition, the Soviet authorities decided to license the production of properly made distilled spirits, and only those that had undergone and passed a rigorous quality-checking procedure were authorized for sale. The green mark was their badge of commercial respectability.

Zelenaya Marka is the flagship brand of the giant Rosskiy Alkogol (Russian Alcohol) group, founded in 2003. Its rise in the market has been meteoric, to the extent that it is now the leading standard brand of vodka stocked in Russian bars. The vodka is produced at the Topaz distillery at Pushkino in the Moscow region, and comes in three variations: Rye, Cedar Nut and Wheat. Water from centuries-old springs goes into the blends, and silver and platinum filters are employed to finish the products.

The Wheat version sold in western markets comes in a rather busily detailed green-labelled bottle, with the original name appearing in transliterated Russian beneath the English.

Taste
Green Mark has a notably soft, gentle nose, dead neutral in the Russian mode, and a distinct soft-water style on the palate. It is rounded, quite bracing, but nicely contoured, and has a very delicate vanilla tone on the sweetish finish. The spirit asserts itself tactfully in the mouth, but then fades beguilingly amid layers of creamy caramel softness.

This makes a fine Black Russian, mixed in equal quantities with Kahlúa, Mexico's coffee liqueur, over plenty of ice.

Made from	Wheat, spring water
ABV	40%
Proof	80
Website	www.rusalco.com/en
Origin	Russia

GREY GOOSE

France is rapidly becoming a major player in the vodka stakes, and Grey Goose is probably its most recognized brand in the export markets. The eagle-eyed will notice that its name is English (it isn't called L'Oie Grise at home), for precisely this reason.

Grey Goose is produced in one of the ancestral homes of distillation, the Cognac region of western France. It is made by essentially the same method as premium brandy, distilled in small batches in a copper pot still, and subjected to a series of five distillations. The water used comes from the artesian springs of Genté in Cognac, and is filtered through limestone from the Grande Champagne district of that region. The process is hawkishly overseen by Grey Goose cellarmaster, François Thibault.

The brand was launched in the United States in 1997, and has established a niche for itself as a connoisseurial product. It has since been extended with a portfolio of three classic flavours.

In design terms, Grey Goose offers more of a Scandinavian than a French archetype, with an image of a flock of the eponymous birds flying over a mountain lake, depicted in cool blue on a frosted bottle. The flavoured versions add bulky images of their respective fruits into the foreground of the aquatic image.

Taste
The neutral vodka has a strong grainy nose, with notes of toasted wheat, which open up on the very complex, attractive palate into all sorts of spicy sensations, most notably caraway and coriander seed. In keeping with the quintuple distillation, there is a caramelly softness and sweetness to the spirit, which sustains it through to a gently rounded finish.

For the flavoured variants, we revert to the language of origin. **Le Citron** (lemon) has pure sherbet-lemon on the nose, and a delicious palate that combines the sharpness of lemon zest with lively citric freshness, to make a great mixing vodka. The lemons used are from the Provençal coastal town of

Made from	Wheat, spring water
ABV	40%
Proof	80
Website	www.greygoose.com
Origin	France

Menton, not far from the Italian border. **L'Orange** has the scent of orange jelly cubes, with a suggestion of the bitter oranges used in Grand Marnier (they're actually from Florida) on the palate. **La Poire** (pear) is my personal favourite. The slight hint of white winegums in the aroma quickly gives way to a palate that is redolent of freshly pressed juicy-ripe pears, the Anjou variety from the Loire Valley.

HUZZAR

Cultural signifiers of the Slavic past abound in the world of vodka, and this one recalls medieval cavalry officers, or hussars, with their ornate uniforms and skilled swordsmanship. Huzzar was launched in 1969, and is now the second biggest vodka brand in the Irish Republic (after Boru, see page 58).

Following a triple distillation (as is also traditional for Ireland's premier spirit, whiskey), the grain spirit is blended with Irish spring water. The mixture is filtered through silver birch charcoal, and is then reduced to below freezing point (–4°C), before being further filtered in its ice-cold state – a process exclusive to this brand.

An ingenious bottle design incorporates a series of diagonal cuts in the glass, intended to evoke the slashing swords of the hussars.

Taste
Despite the violent imagery, Huzzar is a perfectly peaceable customer, with a very shy aromatic profile (barely even spirity). The palate is a little crisper and spikier, with edgy alcohol coming through, and finishing fresh, crisp and bracing.

Its best mixing partners are those with some cutting edge, such as pressed lemon or lime juices. It's good with grapefruit juice, and in a Cosmopolitan. The manufacturers pair it with a range of liqueurs, such as cherry or butterscotch, for some enlivening shots.

Made from	Grain, spring water
ABV	37.5%
Proof	75
Website	www.irishdistillers.ie/ brands/huzzar.shtml
Origin	Ireland

ICEBERG

In the crowded, competitive market of premium vodka, you have to have something that makes you stand out from the encircling throng. How about being able to state that one of the principal ingredients of your product is 12,000 years old?

The clue is in the name, as the blending material in Canada's Iceberg vodka consists of primordially pure water derived from millennia-old icebergs from the Arctic. The brand debuted in 1995, and immediately became one of the spirit world's great stories. The same manufacturer now also makes an Iceberg Gin.

Small icebergs, known as 'growlers', break away from the larger masses in Canada's Arctic north, and then drift southwards through the northern Atlantic Ocean toward the coast of Newfoundland. There, they are harvested by fishermen pursuing a resourceful sideline, delivered to the distiller and melted down into the pure water from which they are formed. This melted water is blended with a triple-distilled spirit made from sweet Canadian corn grown in the province of Ontario.

A gorgeous bottle design suggests a large shard of ice, its serrations fitting smoothly into the hand, and the blue label is evocative of the preternatural blueness of Arctic icebergs.

Taste
The vodka has a very fresh, assertive nose that is full of character. There is a zesty, spritzy lime-and-lemon aromatic quality to it, which is followed through on a light, graceful, highly attractive palate. It's packed with refreshing citric zip buoyed up by nicely rounded spirit, leading to a fresh, light-bodied finish – a class act.

Its fruity complexity makes it an ideal cocktail ingredient, and the sky appears to be the limit, if the producer's own recipe suggestions on the website are anything to go by. Iceberg Citrus Twist involves Iceberg, lychee liqueur, peppermint schnapps, blue curaçao, a nip of cream and a splash of

Made from	Corn, Arctic iceberg water
ABV	40%
Proof	80
Website	www.icebergvodka.com
Origin	Canada

lemon juice. It also crops up as the invigorating element in a spicy, creamy tomato sauce to accompany pasta. Dare one suggest Iceberg is also great on its own, over ice with a twist of lemon or lime?

JEAN-MARC XO

Ascending gracefully into Luxury Land, we find France's Jean-Marc XO, an artisanal vodka made in the Cognac region with all the reverent attention to detail that is traditionally lavished on the fine brandies that are the country's ancestral spirits. In every sense, this is an east European archetype translated into the elegant French idiom.

It is made from four rare varieties of French wheat. For the record, these are: Ysengrain, Orvantis, Azteque and Chargeur. The spirit produced from them is subjected to no fewer than nine distillations in very small batches in copper stills. It is also given a gentle micro-oxygenation, a practice accorded to certain quality wines, in which streams of tiny bubbles are blown through the liquid, which lends suppleness and smoothness to the finished product.

Gensac is the spring water of the Cognac region, filtered naturally through layers of sedimentary limestone. Once blended with the spirit, the mixture is then charcoal-filtered through the burned wood of Limousin oak, the variety used for cognac casks (and also in some winemaking).

The product is the 1990s brainchild of Jean-Marc Daucourt, whose family has for generations been involved in the production of hand-crafted wines and spirits – though not hitherto of vodka.

Each serial-numbered bottle bears the founder's signature, beneath a weighty stopper top, with the XO (a term borrowed from brandy classification, denoting the longest-aged spirits) logo imprinted in letters that fill the bottle. It looks, just as many another super-premium does, like a gigantic bottle of *parfum*.

Taste
The aroma is exceptionally soft and inviting, mixing light caramel with a touch of vanilla and even something like brand-new manila envelopes. The palate is miraculously soft and creamy, the spirit emerging through it with gently understated power. Finishing with rounded, delicately spicy notes (cinnamon?), it all adds up to a supremely well-balanced vodka.

Made from	Wheat, Gensac spring water
ABV	40%
Proof	80
Website	www.jmxo.com
Origin	France

This is a premium product that demands appreciation on its own. I might be inclined even to forgo the ice, just chill it lightly and serve it in small shot-glasses as an accompaniment to aperitif nibbles.

Jean-Marc ®

XO
VODKA

Hand Crafted

DISTILLED FROM FOUR SELECT VARIETIES
OF THE VERY FINEST FRENCH WHEAT FOR
A HARMONIOUS & COMPLEX TASTE

70 cl - 40% vol. - 40% alc./Vol.

PRODUIT DE FRANCE

N° 3771A

JEWEL OF RUSSIA

Many of the premium Russian brands aim explicitly for the highly refined, characterful style of vodka that developed in the late nineteenth century. This was the heyday of the connoisseurial approach to vodka, when it was sipped meditatively from ornamental glasses, and appreciated for the smoothness of its texture and the evanescent flavours it acquired from the grain.

The presence of rye in a vodka always lends it a richer mouth-feel than vodkas made purely from wheat or barley, and the hardiest strains of Russian winter rye and wheat are used in Jewel of Russia. Its water comes from deep-lying artesian wells. Filtration takes place in five separate stages, using a slow-flow process through charcoal made from the stones of peaches and apricots. Further rectification is practised on the super-premium Ultra bottling, in which every attempt is made to ensure the elimination of all congeneric elements, leaving a spirit of exceptional purity.

Just as the production of this vodka reflects the golden age of Russian distillation, so the packaging aims for a classical image. A straight-sided, high-shouldered bottle is inspired by the styles of 300 years ago, while export bottlings for the US market are adorned with red sealing-wax and a silk cord. The Ultra comes in a hand-painted bottle signed by the artist, with a black domed cap that suggests the onion domes of St Basil's Cathedral in Moscow.

Taste

The **Classic** bottling has a strong spirity nose distinguished by a purity of finish like brushed steel. Its squeaky-clean palate makes this a very grown-up style. There are distant hints of aniseed, but the emphasis is on strong, pure alcohol, making it a textbook style of historic Russian vodka. The **Ultra** is an immediately recognizable close relative of the Classic, but smoother still, sweetish in its purity, luxuriously rounded but antiseptically neutral in flavour impact, while the finish offers a big velvet-glove punch of powerful spirit (it's actually the same strength, 40% abv, as the Classic).

Made from	Wheat and rye, artesian spring water
ABV	40%
Proof	80
Website	www.jewelofrussia.com
Origin	Russia

Two flavour variants are offered in certain markets: **Berry Infusion** (cranberries) and **Wild Bilberry Infusion** are both made with hand-picked wild berries that are crushed and macerated in the vodka. The fruit flavours are very intense, but the alcohol content of these products has been adjusted down to 20% for the Berry and 22% for the Bilberry.

KASZTELANSKA

Kasztelanska is something of a rarity, one of the very few cask-aged vodkas available. There are vodkas that pass through casks at some stage in their production, but aging in wood is a procedure much more familiar to whisky and brandy cognoscenti. Over the period they spend in cask, they pick up a natural tawny hue from the wood.

There are two grades. Even the less venerable one is aged for 15 years, but the true connoisseur's version, self-confidently awarded the designation 'Excellent' on the label, has been given no less than 25 years in wood, and is further enriched with wine and fruit extracts. It comes in an escutcheon-shaped bottle with a large, four-sided glass stopper and a label bearing a red seal. You might find the bottle needs extra-careful handling, as it tends to be a little unstable on its tapered base. The bottle is packed in a red-lined wooden presentation box.

Taste
A pale brownish-tawny in hue, Kasztelanska Excellent looks and smells a little like a malt whisky. It has that woody, iodiney nose familiar to Scotch drinkers, with a hint of oxidation from its quarter-century in the barrel. On the palate, it is appealingly light and grainy, with gentle spirit, and with that persistent iodine note of Highland Scotch. Purists may find it difficult to see the point of this style, if we accept the basic premise that vodka is traditionally a completely pure spirit, but it is nonetheless a conscientiously well-made product.

It should be drunk neat, without ice or mixers, as an after-dinner sipper.

Made from	Grains, spring water
ABV	40%
Proof	80
Website	www.polmos.mrrau.net/ home-en.html
Origin	Poland

KAUFFMAN

There's a premium category for upmarket products, there's a super-premium one, and then just occasionally a brand comes along that insists on having a category all to itself. Such is Kauffman, a Russian vodka for the twenty-first century, and for people who at the very least own an oil well or two.

This vodka is the creation of Dr Mark Kaufman [sic], a Russian entrepreneur whose taste for the good things in life – among them gourmet cuisine and fine wines – led him to investigate the possibilities in producing a vodka that would take its place alongside the top XO cognacs and Grand Cru wines at the rarefied end of the marketplace.

There are two Kauffmans, Collection and Private Collection. Together, they represent a marketing innovation, in that this brand is the world's first example of a vintage-dated vodka, its debut release being the 2002. Each bottle is the product of a single year's wheat harvest from some of Russia's premier cereal-growing regions.

The vodka is produced in small batches under the micro-management of a master distiller, and only one bottling is carried out in any vintage. Around 5000 cases of the Collection are produced each year, with about 2700 cases of the Private Collection.

Great pains have been taken over the packaging. Collection comes in a curvaceous bottle that tapers toward the bottom before flaring out again to the base. The large silver top common to both bottlings is pointed on the left side, giving it the silhouette of an exotic bird sitting on its perch. The Private Collection arrives in a large, square white box, which splits down the middle to reveal a rounded, flask-shaped bottle emerging – like Botticelli's Venus – from a silky lining of nacreous white.

Taste
An interesting, complex, spice-toned nose is the first impression of the **Collection**, with hints of clove, cassia, even ginger. It is wondrously soft and sweet on entry, caramelly, with overtones of light toffee and vanilla reflecting

Made from	Wheat from a single year
ABV	40%
Proof	80
Website	www.vodkakauffman.com
Origin	Russia

the gossamer touch of the spirit. Nobody could argue with its obvious pedigree.

The **Private Collection** (both samples I tasted were the 2005) has an initially quite neutral nose in comparison to its stablemate, but then gentle green touches come through, a little cucumber rind, a little basil. It is so miraculously soft on the palate, it's virtually like pure spring water, leaving the mouth fresh and just gently caressed by something powerful. This is about as silky as a 40% spirit is capable of getting, and quite an achievement.

It would be idiotic to mask the painstaking subtlety of these vodkas with mixers. Indeed, they only need gently chilling, certainly not bunging in the freezer. Whether they are worth the formidable price of admission can only be for each consumer to decide, but their stunning quality is not in any doubt.

KETEL ONE

You may think that the countries of north-west Europe would be relatively new to the vodka game, but the lineage of Ketel One can be traced back to the end of the seventeenth century. It was in 1691 that Joannes Nolet (1638–1702) founded a family distillery in the city of Schiedam in South Holland. In a rare example of unbroken patrimony in the distillation business, his direct tenth-generation descendant, Carolus Nolet, still oversees the vodka production.

In a country more readily associated with the making of gin (which Nolet also produces), Dutch vodka has always been a niche product. Ketel One is so named for the copper pot still (or *ketel* in Dutch) used in the production. The name refers to the oldest copper pot in use to this day at the distillery, Distilleerketel #1, which was installed in 1864, and still occupies pride of place among its younger cousins. The grain base of Ketel One is wheat, and the spirit is purified with a gentle charcoal filtration, the passage taking place without pumping, but solely by the force of gravity.

The aim of the current generation of the Nolet family was to create a vodka that makes a distinguished foundation for classic mixed drinks. While the neutral version is held to be a fine base for a vodka martini, the flavoured Citroen, which is infused with lemon and lime extracts, is expressly designed for today's fruity cocktails such as Cosmopolitan.

A fairly classic bottle design offers a chattily informative label, surmounted by a historic illustration of a distillery worker shovelling coal into the fire beneath the old *ketel*.

Taste

The plain vodka has an assertive, grainy nose, leading to a rich, toasted-wheat palate surrounded by beautifully streamlined alcohol, with no sharp edges. It follows through to a soft, sustained finish, which shows a little biscuity character in the aftertaste.

Made from	Wheat
ABV	40%
Proof	80
Website	www.ketelone.com
Origin	Netherlands

In the **Citroen**, concentrated lemon flavours predominate, but with the suggestion of a citrus-based dessert such as lemon tart, the rich wheatiness of the spirit now hinting at short pastry. Indeed, the alcohol seems distinctly gentler on the finish than is the case with a lot of flavoured vodkas.

KOSKENKORVA

Koskenkorva ('the place by the rapids' in rough translation) is the name of a small village in the district of Ilmajoki in western Finland, where this vodka originally hails from. The most widely consumed clear spirit brand in Finland, it is only on export markets that it tends to be known as a vodka, its producers preferring the generic term *viina*, which denotes any ardent spirit, on its home territory. The home bottling is slightly lower in strength (38% abv).

Koskenkorva is produced in Helsinki by the state-owned distiller, Altia, and was created as a brand in 1953. Should you find yourself in a bar in Finland and wish to order a tot, it might be useful to know that it is affectionately referred to as Kossu.

It is produced from Finnish six-row barley, the cultivation of which is almost exclusively sustained by Altia. Pure glacial spring water that requires no filtration is used to dilute it, and it also has a modicum of sugar added to it to soften its mouth-feel.

The dead simple European export packaging uses the word 'Vodka' on the label, and also displays the figure 013, Koskenkorva's product registration number. In the USA, a sleeker, more elegant bottle contains just the name in bold black lettering beneath the blue cross of the national flag.

Taste
On the nose, this is a very clean and gentle vodka, opening up in the mouth with a weighty but subtly insinuating presence. There is a little light spice in the flavour and a more assertive suggestion of toasted grains, leading to a big smooth finish.

Among the flavoured versions, **Blueberry** has a perfect blueberry aroma, evocative of crushed fresh, wild berries, but then a slug of something more medicinal on the palate; **Nordic Berry**, an aromatic vodka with an enticing mix of blackberry, loganberry and blueberry on the nose, has a complex, bitter, almost balsamic palate; **Green Apple** has a fabulous scent of crisp,

Made from	Six-row barley, glacial spring water
ABV	40%
Proof	80
Website	www.koskenkorva.com
Origin	Finland

tart apple (think Granny Smith), waxy, apple-skin palate and appetizing true fruit character; **Vanilla** has more toffee than vanilla in the aroma, leaving a sweet, rounded, caramelly impression on the palate. These flavoured vodkas are all bottled at 37.5% abv, and the spirit in them is distinctly softer than it is in many of the other flavoured brands.

KREMLYOVSKAYA

Known by the diminutive endearment Kremly wherever it is drunk, this is very much a product of the new Russia that began to dawn toward the end of President Mikhail Gorbachev's era of glasnost. The name may refer to the Kremlin, but the vodka's image is far from the dour Russian hooch of the Soviet era; instead, it aims to take its place in the Western wonderland with niche marketing and a proliferating range of flavour offshoots.

Established in 1991, Kremlyovskaya is made in the Russian exclave of Kaliningrad (formerly Königsberg) from a blend of two types of grain – wheat and traditional Russian rye. The latter always makes for a richer, grainier-tasting spirit, but the blend with wheat enables its producers to make a convincing compromise style that won't prove a jolt to western palates. It is triple-distilled for purity and smoothness, and is then subjected to a painstakingly elaborate 12-stage filtration procedure. It is positioned as a premium product for drinking neat in shot-glasses.

After some legal wrangling in Moscow in 2008 over whether the brand had the right to use an image of the Kremlin towers (principally the Spasskaya Tower) on its label, where they are depicted in gold beneath an overarching red brand name on frosted glass, the product is once more off and running in foreign markets. In Russia itself, it remains very much an aspirational product, with just a tiny share of the market.

Range extension has been bullish, with a portfolio of attractive fruit variants now numbering Plum, Melon, Grapefruit, Apricot and Blackcurrant, which are joined by Vanilla and – a reference brand of the contemporary cocktail set – Chocolate.

Taste
The original Kremly is mineral-fresh in the glass, with definite notes of rye bread softly materializing on the palate. Its alcohol impact is both powerful and silky, tenderly gentle as it coats the tastebuds, but with forthright spirity authority on the finish.

Made from	Wheat and rye, spring water
ABV	40%
Proof	80
Website	www.spi-group.com
Origin	Russia

Among the flavoured versions, the **Chocolate** is undoubtedly the standout product, and worth seeking out for its rich, adult, Belgian-chocolate tones, and complex suggestions of vanilla and coffee in the flavour.

KROLEWSKA

Although its image plays on aspects of royal Polish history, Królewska is a relatively new brand, having been launched by the state-owned Polmos combine in the mid-1990s. It is produced at Zielona Góra, a small city in the region of Lower Silesia in western Poland, whose name means 'green mountain'.

A vodka made in the traditional style, Królewska is produced from selected strains of Polish rye, with pure spring water added. It is distilled four times, and then subjected to an elaborate multi-stage rectification and filtration process. The result is a vodka that combines the richness of a rye spirit with the ethereal purity of an elevated premium product.

In an era when Poland can afford to be relaxed about its feudal, monarchial past, Królewska is an unashamed exercise in cultural nostalgia. The brand name is derived from the Polish word for 'royal', *krolewski*. The southern city of Kraków was the seat of the Polish royal family and the country's capital between the eleventh and sixteenth centuries.

The tall frosted bottle with its flared base vaguely resembles a space rocket, but the cultural referencing of the label is steeped in centuries-old history. It is a reproduction of a stained-glass window from the fourteenth-century Mariacki (St Mary's) basilica in Kraków's Grand Square, possibly the most famous church in all of Poland. Reading downwards, the three panels of the window depict the royal coat of arms, the crowned white eagle, and the triple turrets of the old city of Kraków. The eagle has been a proud symbol of Polish autonomy since medieval times. During the communist period between 1945 and 1989 it was retained as the national emblem, but its crown was unceremoniously removed.

Taste

There is a brisk, fresh, almost ozone quality to the nose, like filling your lungs with sea air. The palate is clean and pure, with a distinct note of liquorice underpinned by fleeting hints of caraway. It finishes with the streamlined, muscular impact of a powerful spirit. This is a good vodka to drink neat, but it also mixes well with pressed fruit juices such as apple and grapefruit.

Made from	Rye, spring water
ABV	40%
Proof	80
Origin	Poland

KRUPNIK

Fruits are not the only additive used in producing the traditional flavoured vodkas of Poland. The tradition of *krupnik*, or honey vodka, has its origins in the pre-distillation period in the thirteenth century, when honey was added to mulled beer or wine, and fermented honey products such as mead and *czemiga* (a kind of hydromel, or fermented diluted honey) were infused with herbs and spices to make healthy or warming cordials.

Honey was an obvious fermentation material, being so full of natural sugars. It could be used to make kvass, the everyday light rye beer, or mead – richer and higher in alcohol. This was a festive drink for special occasions, and was often spiced, or had fruits macerated in it. Another speciality was *trojniak pomorski*, produced in Pomerania since the twelfth century, a mixture of beer and honey water, flavoured with spices such as cardamom and ginger and berries such as juniper and dried raspberries.

As elsewhere in Europe, honey was the principal sweetener before the arrival of sugar from the West Indies. It was used as a preserving medium, in baking, and for dressing fresh fruit. One technique involved cooking wild berries in honey, then drying the resulting mixture in layered sheets to make a kind of fruity toffee.

The Starograd distillery of Gdansk makes the *krupnik* pictured here. It is labelled as a 'Polish honey liqueur', rather than a vodka, but it is nonetheless vodka-based. It is made with wild honey, together with infusions of many herbs and spices, including cinnamon and nutmeg, to a recipe from south-east Poland that dates back to the eighteenth century.

Taste
A delicate straw-yellow in colour, the nose speaks of something savoury preserved in honey. The herbal aromatics lend it a medicinal air, recalling the age-old use of honey in comforting cold remedies. On the palate, despite its gentle sweetness, it is very definitely an adult taste, full of bitter and complex spice notes, and its alcohol (38% in Poland, 40% for export) is seamlessly integrated into the overall composition.

Made from	Grain, honey, herbs, spices
ABV	40%
Proof	80
Origin	Poland

As one would expect, honey vodka blends well with lemonade, and a spoonful added to a glass of champagne makes a rather luxurious wintertime aperitif.

LITHUANIAN ORIGINAL

The history of Lithuanian vodka is almost entirely encapsulated in the Stumbras company, which produces this and other vodkas listed in this book (see Ozone, page 142 and Stumbras, page 184). It was founded in 1906 when the country was a constituent part of Tsarist Russia, at a time when vodka production was subject to the strictest state controls. In quality terms, then, it could be said that its founders started as they meant to go on.

The premises were ravaged by German occupying forces during the Great War. With the armistice, Lithuania regained its independence and Stumbras re-emerged into the daylight, helped by the investments of certain wealthy families; the company diversified into liqueurs, bitters and brandies, as well as the ancestral vodka. The plant flourished after Lithuania's absorption into the USSR, when Soviet researchers revived many age-old recipes for traditional aromatized spirits. In 2003, the company moved seamlessly into private management.

A continuous triple distillation in column stills is followed by careful removal of trace impurities, in the procedure known as rectification. The spirit is then blended with water that has undergone a six-fold filtering, followed by the painstakingly slow filtration of the final composition through crushed quartz and activated birchwood charcoal.

Taste

The **Original Classic** bottling has a very discreet aromatic profile, being much less assertive than its Stumbras stablemates. This is definitely the Russian-influenced pure style. Aniseed and mint emerge on the palate, supported by the unmistakable taste of ultra-purified water and clean, self-effacing alcohol.

The premium **Gold** has the telltale nose of highly purified vodka, very clean, with only the most subliminal waft of spirit. Its richly smooth palate evokes mocha coffee and caramel in a luxuriously soft, satiny medium, the alcohol only showing through at the end. Even the **Stipri** (Strong) bottling, at 45%, is bracingly pure, like mountain spring water with just the faintest

Made from	Grain, filtered water
ABV	40%
Proof	80
Website	www.stumbras.eu/en/ products?folder=4
Origin	Lithuania

smoulder of spirit. The dead-neutral palate is soft and smooth, the alcohol hit impressively kid-glove. It's intensely warm but well-balanced.

The flavoured range is equally admirable, using natural juices for flavour and colour, and with a handful of whole berries in each bottle. **Raspberry** is creamily aromatic, with sweetly ripe fruit on a dry, neutral spirit base. **Cherry** smells of cherry jam, cherry brandy and cherry stones, while **Cranberry** has a fantastic berry nose that suggests blueberries too, and the flavour of berry compote, with a complex, medicinal note and a long, gently bitter finish. **Blackcurrant**, **Bilberry** and **Pepper and Honey** complete the range. These are bottled at 40% at home, but 35% on the export markets.

LUKSUSOWA

Luksusowa is one of the more venerable names in Polish vodka. Known as a brand since 1928, its name is derived directly from its quality level, which denotes the highest – therefore most 'luxurious' – state of purity. It claims an impressive 10% of the domestic vodka market in Poland, which is not bad going for a high-end product.

Although popularly associated with potatoes, most commercial vodka is made from grains of one sort or another. The real potato vodkas have therefore attained something of the aura of the speciality product, particularly when made in Poland, arguably the ancestral home of potato spirits. Banish all thoughts of Irish poteen, its roughness and readiness. Properly made potato vodka is an experience all its own.

Luksusowa is made from potatoes grown in the richly fertile loam of northern Poland's Baltic coast. The vodka is triple-distilled to create a smooth, streamlined spirit, and then filtered through activated charcoal for purity. Fine spring water is used for blending. The whole process takes place at the vodka's home since the 1920s in Zielona Góra, in the west of the country.

The neutral vodka comes in two strengths – 40% and 50% – as well as a trio of flavoured versions: Dzika Jeżyna (Wild Blackberry), Miodowa Tradycyjna (Traditional Honey) and Żurawina (Cranberry), the first two launched in 2006, the last in 2007.

A narrow red strip of a label on a square-sided bottle is surmounted by the Polish eagle in red set in a Gothic arch.

Taste
The nose is less pungently aromatic than some potato vodkas, displaying instead the clean neutrality of a triple-distilled spirit. It is sweetish and creamy on entry to the palate, less lumpy in texture than other potato brands, and with relatively gentle alcohol on the finish. The higher-strength version is all subdued power. A laconic advertising slogan, 'Nothing To Add', indicates that these vodkas are made for drinking as neat shots straight from the freezer.

Made from	Potatoes
ABV	40%
Proof	80
Origin	Poland

MOSKOVSKAYA

This, more than any other Russian prototype, is the vodka for purists. It has been made outside Russia from time to time in recent years (in Ukraine typically), and is now bottled in Latvia, but the blueprint remains unimpeachable. For many authorities, and certainly those less inclined to accept Poland's case for primacy in vodka history, this is the reference brand, and one of the three biggest in the world.

Founded in 1901 at the Moscow State Distillery No 1, it supplied the Kremlin through both Tsarist times and Soviet, with the finest grades – usually labelled Cristall – of ultra-pure grain spirit. A break in production occurred during the First World War and in the early years of the Bolshevik regime, but the distillery was relicensed in 1925 after Lenin's death.

Entitlement to the brand name has been endlessly contested since the winding-up of the USSR. A successor company to the old Soviet drinks export monopoly, Soyuzplodimport, has so far fruitlessly tried to wrest the brand name from the privately owned SPI Group, which is responsible for all of the Moskovskaya imported into western Europe. The distinctive, old-fashioned green label and the all-important description Moskovskaya Osobaya (Moscow Special) are the constants in the drink's history – together with the use of pure spring water, rather than distilled water, to ensure a lively texture. The vodka featured here is the SPI product.

Taste
There is a lovely elemental purity about the vodka. One sniff confirms it to be as pure as virgin snow; on the palate, it is generously rounded and gorgeously soft, with hardly any alcohol burn at all. It is virtually the perfect neutral Russian style, and as such makes a flawless neat tipple, especially when served, as intended, with Russian zakuski (see page 38).

Made from	Wheat, artesian spring water
ABV	40%
Proof	80
Website	www.moskovskaya.com
Origin	Russia

NEMIROFF

Now enjoying around a third of the spirits market in its native territory, Ukraine's Nemiroff is a fast-rising brand. It is named after a village, Nemyriv, in the heartland of the Vinnytsia region south-west of Kiev. This fertile agricultural area was settled by the Scythians in antiquity, and had become an important cultural centre by the Middle Ages. Records of a drink recognizable as vodka being produced there date back to the middle of the eighteenth century.

The composition of Nemiroff is unusual. Distilled from high-grade wheat and mixed with purified water pumped from artesian wells, the spirit undergoes filtration through charcoal before the addition of its special ingredients, dried caraway seeds and painstakingly selected light-coloured varieties of honey. These don't turn it into a flavoured vodka as such, but enhance and deepen the flavour range of what is essentially a neutral vodka.

Nemiroff Original, or Nemiroff Black as its international aficionados have come to know it since its launch in 1999, comes in a tall, four-sided bottle, with the brand name spelled out vertically in gold on the label and embossed in the glass on the side of the bottle. The producers consider this to be a particularly masculine type of vodka, and the styling consciously reflects that positioning.

Taste
This is an extremely discreet vodka aromatically, with virtually no trace of scent, hardly even any impression of alcohol, which speaks of its high degree of rectification. Take a sip, though, and a whole new world opens up. It has a lush, creamy entry on to the palate, with notes of toasted cereal grains enrobed in caramelized softness. The spirit comes through strongly at the end, but overall the product shows exemplary balance.

The range is extended with **Light** (a 38% bottling containing cardamom), **Strong** (50%, with hops, caraway and honey), **Premium** (for which additional purification is reserved), and a super-premium, **Lex** (from the Latin word for 'law', denoting a product aimed at those who are a law unto them-

Made from	Wheat, artesian spring water, honey, botanicals
ABV	40%
Proof	80
Website	www.nemiroff.ua
Origin	Ukraine

selves). This last is based on spirit that has been treated to a six-month maturation before the water is added. Flavour variants include **Honey-Pepper**, **Rye Honey**, **Birch Buds**, **Cranberry**, **Citron**, **Lime** and **Currant** (blackcurrant).

OVAL

In the world of concept vodkas, Austria's Oval has set new standards. Its packaging, production technique and – most importantly – its taste have broken new ground and catapulted Austria (previously noted for beer, wine and the odd liqueur) into the spirits limelight.

The key notion we are introduced to here is 'structure'. This is the world's first 'structured' vodka, and its manufacturers claim to have made a breakthrough in the preparation of distilled spirits. The spirit and the water are prepared entirely separately in a process that takes place over several days, the former triple-distilled and rectified in a column apparatus, the latter purified by osmosis (diffusion through a semi-permeable membrane) and demineralized.

The two ingredients are then gradually blended in a temperature-controlled environment, which produces a crystalline molecular structure, with the water molecules surrounding the alcohol molecule in the form of a tetrahedron. According to the manufacturer, it is this final state, the product of combined Russian and Austrian scientific investigation, that accounts for the particularly pleasing texture of the finished vodka.

Made just south of Vienna, Oval is bottled at three strengths: 24% abv (described as a 'structured vodka based spirit' as it is below the EU legal minimum of 37.5%), 42%, and the true aficionado's 56%. There is also an amber-coloured Vogelbeere (Rowanberry) version, naturally flavoured with the gently bitter little scarlet berries of the rowan tree.

If plenty of care is lavished on the vodka itself, it should come as no surprise to see that the bottle is also a design masterpiece (and an award-winning one too). Reflecting the tetrahedral molecular structure of the spirit within, it looks like an outsize eau de toilette bottle, complete with glass stopper, and would grace any upmarket drinks cabinet. Handle with care.

Taste
So what has all this painstaking scientific research and design effort produced? The 42% bottling offers a thrilling, subtle smoulder to the nose, which makes

Made from	Wheat, water purified by osmosis
ABV	42%
Proof	84
Website	www.oval-vodka.com
Origin	Austria

its entry on to the palate all the more extraordinary, for the unexpected smoothness, sweetness and softness with which it slips over the taste buds. Its rich, lightly grainy flavours build up to a big, savoury finish. Serve moderately, but not agonizingly, chilled with ice and a twist of lemon.

42

OVAL

STRUCTURED VODKA

DISTILLED FROM GRAIN
42% ALC. BY VOL.

OZONE

The Stumbras company is the primary distiller in Lithuania, with a proud tradition reaching back to the dying days of the Tsarist era in 1906. (For more on its history, see the entry for Lithuanian Original.) It makes a versatile range of neutral and flavoured vodkas, as well as brandies, bitters and liqueurs, in the traditional style, but has also kept a vigilant eye on modern market trends, as is evidenced by the premium bottling, Ozone.

Aimed at the new generation of vodka drinkers in western style bars, Ozone comes in a minimalist designer bottle, the signature O logo shown in floating bubbles of red and silver. The ingenious closure features a pop-top, which is activated when the capsule is turned. Within a couple of years of its launch, it was winning medals at international drinks competitions.

Taste
A mellow, immensely subtle aromatic profile offers up fugitive hints of caramel, giving way to gentle, toasty wheatiness on the palate. The spirit component is reasonably assertive but not at all harsh-edged, making for an attractive, pretty neutral, antiseptically clean style.

This vodka would make a fine, vigorously chilled neat shot, with ice and a twist of lemon, but it is also a resourceful mixer, insinuating its way silkily into blends with orange or apple juices, and fruit-juicy cocktails such as Sea Breeze.

A first flavour variant, **Ozone Vodka and Melon**, was launched in 2006 to coincide with the centenary of the Stumbras company. Bottled at 38% abv, it has a richly defined green melon flavour that works well with pineapple juice, and also as a shot in a glass of sparkling wine. Stumbras also recommends it in an equal-parts mix with your favourite energy drink, and a wedge of lime.

Made from	Wheat, filtered water
ABV	40%
Proof	80
Website	www.stumbras.eu
Origin	Lithuania

PIEPRZOWKA

Like all the traditional eastern European flavours, pepper vodka has its origins in the need to mask the off-putting taste of raw, unrectified spirit when distillation was still comparatively little understood. Along with herbs, fruits, nuts and flowers, spices were pressed into service for the assertive character they could lend to an otherwise rank spirit.

Exactly when pepper vodkas were first systematically produced may never be known, but we do know that Peter the Great (Tsar Peter I, who reigned from 1682 to 1725) enjoyed flavoured vodkas. His own declared preference was for a triple-distilled vodka that was diluted with aniseed water and then distilled again, but he also favoured the technique of seasoning a glass of fine vodka with pepper.

By the time their production methods had become refined, these flavoured products were usually based on quadruple- or even quintuple-distilled spirit, in which various plant extracts were steeped. They were expensive to produce and were confined to the rarefied orders of society; after the eighteenth century, their unprofitability led them into a period of gentle decline.

Interestingly, in Russia at least, the term 'vodka' was initially employed specifically for these aromatized products, as distinct from neutral vodka, which was still imprecisely referred to as *vino*.

The pepper vodka tradition spread from Russia, where it is known as *pertsovka*, through Ukraine, which has its *Ukrainskaya s pertsem*, and Poland, where it is known as *pieprzówa* or *pieprzówka*. All are distinguished by the spicy catch in the flavour, which can be anything from a warming tingle to a vice-like grip at the back of the throat. They are considered, logically enough, to be particularly useful in a classic Bloody Mary mix, where they help to turn up the heat for those who like an especially spicy concoction.

Polmos Lubuska in western Poland produces one of the most widely seen Polish examples on export markets. Based on twice-rectified spirit, it contains essence of Turkish pepper, paprika and dashes of other spirits, namely rum

Made from	Grains, pepper essence, paprika, chillies, peppercorns, cubebs etc.
ABV	45%
Proof	90
Origin	Poland

and apple brandy. The drink is a highly improbable-looking shocking pink, a colour not seen in nature. It comes in a bottle with a fiery red label, and an image of a red chilli pepper bush. The name is given in French (*vodka au poivre*) as well as in Polish.

Taste

This example of Pieprzówka has surprisingly little scent for a pepper vodka, but the palate is insistently peppery. Its high alcohol content (45%) ramps up the heat effect, and there is a minty topnote as well. That strong spirit then helps the spice to come burning through at the end.

PINKY

Launched in 2002, Sweden's Pinky is an attempt to light out into new territory. It's something between a plain and a flavoured vodka, a neutral grain spirit that has been sensitively aromatized and coloured with a bouquet of botanical ingredients.

The vodka base is made from hardy Swedish winter wheat, distilled a thoroughgoing five times and then reduced to drinking strength with pure glacial meltwater. A dozen botanical components are then blended in by hand, practically in the manner of a premium gin. Principal among these are violets and rose petals, which lend the drink an uplifting floral perfume, while wild strawberries add an attractive summer-fruit touch. The spirit is naturally high in esters, chemical compounds evolved during distillation, which create those fruity topnotes you find in certain wines.

Pinky was in fact conceived by a panel of wine-tasters, in an attempt to give to a vodka some of the aroma complexes you might find in a rosé wine or champagne. It blends exceptionally well with cranberry juice, and indeed with most other fruit juices, and although it is a soft, naturally achieved shell-pink in colour, the hue is delicate enough not to clash with differently coloured juices.

As with many other premium spirits, the elegant bottle recalls the perfume counter (fittingly in this case). Its tall, square-shouldered profile with discreet black couture-style label suggests contemporary female power-dressing, or the hand-drawn fashion illustrations of the post-war era. In 2008 a commercial tie-in with lingerie label Agent Provocateur helped to seal the vodka's appeal to a certain kind of smart, urban woman.

Taste
Its very delicate pink colour – like the palest types of rosé champagne – is highly appealing. The nose is vivacious and graceful, with a distinct note of strawberry ice-cream, backed up by the discreet but unmistakable presence of rose petal, like real Turkish Delight. It is intensely floral on the palate, with pot-pourri notes, and ends with a firm hit of alcohol that needs taming with the right mixers.

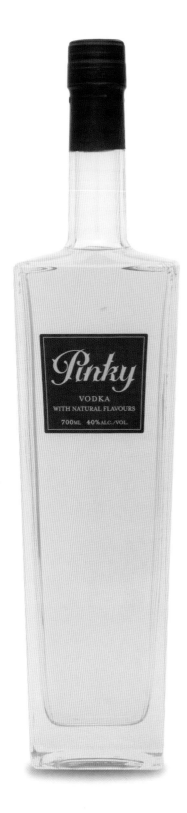

Made from	Wheat, rose petals, violets, wild strawberries, glacial water
ABV	40%
Proof	80
Website	www.pinkyvodka.com
Origin	Sweden

It's very tempting to add a slug to a glass of pink champagne, garnishing the glass with a strawberry on a cocktail stick, or mix it in equal parts with crème de fraise (strawberry liqueur) and top with soda. If only they'd given it a slightly more elegant name…

POLONAISE

Polonaise is one of the premium brands of the Lancut distillery in south-east Poland. Lancut was established in 1784 by Princess Izabela Lubomirska, widow of Prince Stanislaw Lubomirski, who had died two years previously. It quickly gained a reputation for producing the finest plain, aromatized and sweet vodkas in Poland.

The distillery survived in private hands until 1944, when – caught between retreating Nazi occupation forces and the Red Army brigades advancing from the east – it suffered extensive destruction. During the communist era, production was controlled by the state alcohol company, and then, with the formal dissolution of the nationalized Polmos system in 1990–1991, Lancut once more became an independently run business.

Polonaise is named after the Polish national dance, a sedate affair in waltz time, popularized by the works of Chopin. The Polish term *polonez* is adapted from the French word, and probably derives from the time Polish families served their spirits (known to them as *okowita*) to French soldiers of the Napoleonic armies. The soldiers christened it *eau de vie polonaise*, or Polish spirit, and the term passed back into the Polish language.

The bottle comes with an ornate deep blue and silver label, and uses the Polish spelling of 'wódka'.

Taste

Polonaise has aromas in the herbal range, with a touch of mint and light aniseed. On the palate, that anise quality comes through quite assertively, with fairly weighty alcohol presence in a very grown-up style. It's a serious vodka for cold nights, and one that drinks very well neat, owing to the richness of its grain profile.

Made from	Rye, distilled water
ABV	40%
Proof	80
Website	www.polmoslancut.com
Origin	Poland

POTOCKI

The key date in Potocki vodka's history (as a glance at the neck-label indicates) is 1816, which is when Alfred, a scion of the Polish noble family of that name, inherited the magnificent Lancut Castle and its distillery, the second oldest in Poland. Established in 1784, the latter attained its true glory under Alfred and his brother Arthur, producing a range of spirits and liqueurs that were particularly favoured by the Habsburg emperors.

The Potockis' finest hour was in the fifteenth century, when they demonstrated sterling service as defenders of the Polish crown against the successive incursions of Russians, Tatars and Turks. The heraldic symbol that graces the label is a battlefield emblem that commemorates the fearsome martial reputation of the clan.

At the end of the Second World War, the Lancut distillery was requisitioned by the new communist authorities and remained in the possession of the state until the dissolution of the Soviet bloc in 1991. It is now restored to commercial autonomy as Polmos Lancut (see Polonaise, page 148). Meanwhile, Jan-Roman Potocki, a lineal descendant of Alfred, now oversees production of this premium rye vodka at a modest distillation facility in central Poland.

Made in small batches, Potocki is in every sense a hand-crafted product, each batch conscientiously tasted and approved by Jan-Roman and his distiller. Perhaps surprisingly, the rye mash is only twice-distilled and is subjected to no filtration, in order to retain all its innate regional characteristics.

The supremely elegant, rectangular bottle is adorned with a small dark blue label with the family emblem beneath an embossed crown.

Taste

This is for me a desert-island vodka. It has a preternaturally beautiful scent of complex sweetness and richness, almost cocoa-bean in its exoticism, and a palate-coating, classy richness. It is so brimming with character, it's practically like tasting a sophisticated liqueur, with its notes of mocha and coffee, all enveloped in true rye richness. That mouth-filling softness and creaminess

Made from	Rye
ABV	40%
Proof	80
Website	www.potockivodka.com
Origin	Poland

continues through to the gently fading, joyous finish. It absolutely demands to be drunk neat, but well-chilled rather than frozen to preserve its special character.

RAIN ORGANICS

Rain Organics vodka is owned by Sazerac of New Orleans, Louisiana, which began making vodkas in the period immediately after the Second World War. Given that hardly anybody knew how to drink vodka in the West at that time, this was a truly enterprising phenomenon, especially for a company that had its origins in the mid-nineteenth century as an unassuming coffee-house in the French Quarter of the city.

The brand was founded in 1992, when Sazerac purchased a small distilling operation from Buffalo Trace, better known for making bourbon whiskey. An innovative approach to distillation, together with the use of a special yeast strain for the initial mash, were among the unique attributes of this producer, and a pair of master distillers, Gary Gayheart and Harlen Wheatley, were instrumental in helping Sazerac develop its organic brand.

A dedicated 400-hectare (1000-acre) farmstead, Fizzle Flats in Yale, Illinois, produces the organically grown white corn from which Rain is made. The vodka is made in small, painstakingly controlled batches, typically over 20 days, in a procedure that begins with a cold-water fermentation, and goes on to a breathtaking seven separate distillations. It is reduced to bottling strength with pure spring water, before the final filtration is carried out through a combination of charcoal and diamond dust.

The bottle is an eye-catching raindrop shape, made of frosted glass and sealed with a dark blue stopper, with the blue logo incorporating a few droplets of rain.

Taste
Corn is a relatively unusual grain to use on its own in vodka, and the idiosyncratic nature of this brand shows up straight away in its hauntingly attractive nose, which displays all the exotic sweetness (toffee, fudge) of other corn liquors. It is a classic corn spirit on the palate too, with lovely, rounded, soft toffee flavours and beautifully integrated alcohol. There is almost the mellowness of a cask-aged spirit about it, despite the fact that it has undergone no such procedure.

Made from	Organic white corn, spring water
ABV	40%
Proof	80
Website	www.rainvodka.com
Origin	United States

This is a very appealing vodka to drink iced and neat, but it also makes a versatile base for any number of fruity cocktails. One of my favourites is the parent company's own recipe, Singin' In The Rain (but of course), which consists of two parts Rain to one part cherry juice and the merest splash of 7-Up, garnished with a fresh red cherry.

RED SQUARE

There is a very British ironic humour about the positioning of Red Square, from the distilling giant, Halewood International. Its 'Get real' slogan highlights the fact that this isn't intended to be a niche product for which extravagant claims are made. So when we read that it is 'aged in diamond-encrusted ice-barrels', the riposte – 'Get real!' – brings us properly back to earth.

This is a standard grain vodka that has been triple-distilled ('three times is enough,' insist the manufacturers), and then carbon-filtered to achieve as neutral a style as possible. It's a quintessential cocktail vodka, but one that aims to give your palate a gentler ride than the very cheap stuff tends to.

There are two neutral styles, the red-label flagship and a more potent black-label version bottled at 43%. This is described as 'cocktail strength', in recognition of the fact that you will want a bit more oomph to the drink, especially in recipes where the spirit is mixed only with fruit juices and no other alcohol. The two fruit versions are Green Apple and Wild Berry, both 37.5%.

The name may reference Moscow's huge focal square, where Lenin's mausoleum stands, but there are no geographical signifiers on the bottle, just a red square with a non-specific double-headed eagle. The brand isn't pretending to be Russian, after all. It's made just outside Liverpool, England.

Taste
As befits the brand's ethos, the spirit has been rectified to almost no aromatic presence. Though it is a little more forthright on the palate, the style is as close to purely neutral as possible, with perhaps just a touch of evanescent aniseed, before closing on a strong, spirity finish.

Wild Berry, inspired by woodland berries, smells of chewy sweets, with raspberry predominating, and has a faintly medicinal palate, a little like one of the more appealing types of cough linctus. Try it with tonic. **Green Apple** is more Golden Delicious than Granny Smith, and has a fugitive hint of pear too. It tastes fine in a mix with apple juice or lemonade.

Made from	Grain, filtered water
ABV	37.5%
Proof	75
Website	www.redsquarevodka.co.uk
Origin	UK (England)

REYKA

Reyka is produced at Iceland's first vodka distillery. Its name is the Icelandic word for 'steam', and derives from the fact that the production plant is powered, as is much else in that frozen island country, by natural geothermal steam from deep beneath the earth's crust. It's the same force of nature that produces geysers, as well as those hot springs that are among the country's luxuries. Built by William Grant (the Scotch distillers who own the brand), in Borgarnes in western Iceland, this is so far the most northerly distillation facility in the world.

The water with which the spirit is blended is drawn from a 4000-year-old lava field, and is wholly uncontaminated, meaning that it doesn't need any refinement or demineralization before it goes into the vodka. Volcanic rock from the same source is used in a unique system of filtration, which helps to ensure a diamond-bright, ethereally pure final product. The grain used is grown in Scotland, but as more barley is being planted in Iceland itself, the brand may eventually become more self-sufficient in its raw materials.

Like other premium vodkas, Reyka is manufactured in small batches, with each parcel subject to the fine tooth-comb attentions of a master distiller. Much fun is made of this in the company's marketing: the vodka is bottled under eight different capsules, illustrating the various events that may have taken place during the preparation of that particular batch – whether it be an encounter with a seal on the way to the distillery, an Arctic fox wandering into the grounds, or even the chance conjunction of an eagle soaring overhead when the first roses bloom.

Reyka is attempting to take a lot of the po-faced luxuriating out of the marketing of premium vodka. What is in deadly earnest is the aim for unblemished purity, to the extent that there are no cinnamon or pomegranate versions of Reyka. Or, as one of its ad campaigns put it, 'The only flavoured vodka we make is vodka-flavoured vodka'. A broad-based bottle keeps the labelling minimally simple, with the country of origin embossed around the shoulder above an image of the volcanic Mount Hekla.

Made from	Wheat and barley, lava-field water
ABV	40%
Proof	80
Website	www.reykavodka.com
Origin	Iceland

Taste

Its purity is immediately apparent on the nose, and its entry to the palate is delightfully sweet and easy. The alcohol is gently caramel-toned in its softness, leading on to a grainy, more savoury finish with subtle spirit smoulder.

ROBERTO CAVALLI

'The quintessence of pure femininity' is how the vodka of one of Italy's premier couture houses positions itself. There isn't too great a distance in cultural terms between clothing today's style-conscious woman and putting an elegant drink in her hand, and a premium vodka suits the contemporary mood.

For years, this vodka was made exclusively for the founder and his nearest and dearest. Its entry on to the international market has been inspired by the ascendancy of premium vodka in recent years, and it becomes the first vodka to be produced from start to finish entirely within Italy.

This is in every sense an aspirational product, as reflected in the manufacturing process. The grain is grown in a verdant valley in northern Italy where the foothills of the Alps sweep down to the river Po. A four-stage distillation in column stills is followed by a fifth and final pass through a copper pot still to smooth out any remaining edges, and then water from springs on the slopes of Monte Rosa is added. The filtration procedure is carried out through flakes of Italy's world-famous Carrara marble, after which the vodka is bottled in small batches.

Entirely in keeping with the image is one of the more graceful bottle designs of any premium vodka. Conceived by Cavalli himself, it is based on his ideal female silhouette, a tall, broad-shouldered Lauren Bacall of a figure with waspishly narrow waist. A ribbed pattern that curls sensuously around the middle suggests the detailing on a couture evening gown.

Taste
The vodka has an ever-so-subtle nose, with just the lightest suggestion of grain, and the palate is taut and lean in its first impact. Gradually, it opens up with toasted-wheat notes and a seasoning of caraway seed. The spirit is just a little nervy at first but well-balanced, and is sustained through to a surprisingly assertive finish, to ensure that the drink leaves a lasting impression.

Made from	Grain, mountain spring water
ABV	40%
Proof	80
Website	www.robertocavallivodka.com
Origin	Italy

It makes a fine mixer in the kinds of simple, old-fashioned cocktails where quality spirit is expected to shine through, rather than being submerged in a welter of exotic juices. As such, the house formula for a vodka martini – two shots of Cavalli to two drops of Martini Dry vermouth, shaken with ice and garnished with a caper on a stalk – is just about perfection.

ROMANOV

Romanov vodka is one of the fastest-growing brands in the newly lucrative Indian market. Its chic, upscale image was enhanced when, in 2006, Bollywood actress Shilpa Shetty became its brand ambassador.

The brand is owned by the global drinks group UB, and is a stablemate of India's biggest vodka brand, White Mischief (see page 204). The flagship bottling, Romanov, is a snazzily packaged, high-end product based on a triple distillation of mixed grains, with the addition of demineralized water for smoothness and clarity, and finished with a triple filtration. It is made in the Maharashtra region of western India, home of the country's famous sparkling wine, Omar Khayyam.

Its name, printed in vertical lettering along the bottle, derives from the family name of the Tsars of Russia, and much play has been made of the fact that if you say it backwards – *vonamor!* – it sounds almost as though you are demanding another shot.

Taste
The nose on the Premium bottling is very clean and neutral, after the Russian style, but there is much more aromatic presence on the palate, which suggests roasted corn-on-the-cob, seasoned with a mild spicy hint of ground coriander seed. It's quite a complex vodka with clearly evident premium class, finishing with big, self-important spirit crackle in the aftertaste.

Premium Romanov has been joined by a new, multi-distilled niche vodka, **Romanov Red**, made from a cocktail of grains, including rice, barley, bajra (pearl millet) and jowar (sorghum). It was launched in 2008 by a head-turningly scarlet-clad Ms Shetty. There is also a world's-first **Romanov Diet Mate** version, a low-carb variant that contains the herbal extract garcinia, derived from the fruit of the kokum tree, and a couple of flavoured offerings, **Tropical Thrill** and **Green Apple**.

Made from	Mixed grains, demineralized water
ABV	42.8%
Proof	85.6
Origin	India

ROYALTY

The origins of the grandly named Royalty vodka are unexpectedly humble. Its parent company was established by a baker named Hero Jan Hooghoudt in 1888, initially to make genever (Dutch gin), in a basement distillery at Groningen. He died of pneumonia only a decade after the company was founded, and his widow Grietje carried on the business, assisted in due course by her two sons.

Over the generations, the business diversified into herbal bitters, liqueurs, fruit wines and other spirits, and at its centenary in 1988, Hooghoudt became purveyor to the Dutch royal court. When the fourth-generation scion of the family, Bert Hooghoudt, took up the corporate reins in 1993, his succession coincided with the launch of this premium vodka, packaged in Dutch royal-blue glass.

Royalty is made from the pick of the plentiful Dutch wheat harvest, and distilled four times in a column still. Following its rectification and blending with crystal-clear spring water, it is filtered five times through activated carbon. In recent years, the bottled strength has been increased from 37.5% to 40% abv. The steamlined, royal-blue bottle is highly distinctive, with its embossed royal crest below the neckline and sturdy, broad-based design.

Taste
It has a lovely, breezy, ozone-fresh style, as bracing as filling your lungs on a windswept North Sea coast. There's a minty note in the aroma, and the palate profile is beautifully light and subtle. A tasty, aniseed-scented finish leaves a biggish but well-balanced spirit hit. It makes a good mixer with orange or apple juice, but can also be taken as it comes.

The Royalty range is extended with **Lime** (which also contains a dash of lemon), **Red** (flavoured with blood orange), **Dark** (blackcurrant) and **Black** (blackcurrant and guarana, a caffeine-bearing South American herbal remedy). These are coloured, vodka-based liqueurs, and are also supplemented by a non-alcoholic health drink, Royalty Energy, containing caffeine and taurine, a metabolic agent thought to have detoxifying properties.

Made from	Wheat, spring water
ABV	40%
Proof	80
Website	www.royaltyvodka.com www.hooghoudt.nl/en
Origin	Netherlands

RUSSIAN STANDARD

Many of the Russian and Polish vodkas play on heritage themes, but in the case of Russian Standard, its claim to historical lineage is entirely justified. It can be traced back to the work of the great Russian chemist, Dmitri Mendeleev (see page 17), formulator of the periodic table of the elements, whose investigations in the nineteenth century helped to establish new standards for distillation. In 1894, Tsar Alexander III commissioned him to produce a supremely refined vodka for the imperial court, and his formula is still used for all bottlings of Russian Standard.

The vodka is made from robust winter wheat grown on the Russian steppe, blended with the soft glacial meltwater of Lake Ladoga in the ice-bound north. Distillation is carried out at a brand-new facility in St Petersburg, opened in 2006, for which the phrase 'state-of-the-art' is for once justified. Its gleaming silver towers are a landmark of industrial architecture, and the plant is equipped with a 35-m (115-feet) high purification column, as well as various filtration systems for each of the three bottlings.

Original is distilled four times before being charcoal-filtered. Platinum receives six distillations and filtration through silver, while at the top of the tree, Imperia benefits from kid-glove treatment: no fewer than eight distillations and filtration through layers of crystal quartz sourced from the Ural mountains. All three are given a 48-hour 'relaxation' period, which allows them to settle to the optimum, uniform alcohol level of 40%.

The bottle designs aim for a compromise of historic references and contemporary style. Each is distantly suggestive of the shape of a bell, specifically the one in the Peter the Great bell-tower in Moscow. Unusually, and bravely, the brand name is given in the Cyrillic alphabet, and isn't at all obviously decipherable to non-Russian speakers. Imperia has the most futuristic appearance – a faceted version of the bell design, with a long, deep-red capsule.

Made from	Wheat, glacial spring water
ABV	40%
Proof	80
Website	www.russianstandardvodka.com
Origin	Russia

Taste

Original has a fresh, bracing nose, with an equally fresh, sharply etched structure in the mouth. It is full of crystalline purity, overlaid with a faint suggestion of spearmint, which echoes on the finish. **Platinum** has similar cleanliness on the nose, with a more obviously rectified palate, which allows the powerful but mellow spirit to surface. **Imperia** has even sweeter, softer alcohol, with intriguing fresh vegetal notes on the palate, suggestive of newly chopped fennel or celery, and a muscle-flexing finish.

SKYY

California's Skyy brand is a textbook example of Stateside ingenuity. From extremely modest beginnings in 1992, it has blossomed into one of the most sought-after niche drink brands in the United States, with the kind of reputation that many of California's world-renowned boutique wineries have established. Such a trajectory is all the more remarkable in that the intentions of its founder, Maurice Kanbar – to create an exceptionally smooth, clean premium vodka – were scarcely revolutionary.

Skyy is, however, infused with enough of the pioneering spirit to have had a bespoke distillation procedure formulated for it. The vodka is distilled four times in column stills from grain harvested in the American Midwest, and then subjected to a triple filtration for maximum softness and cleanliness. Its manufacturers claim that Skyy has fewer residual impurities than any other leading premium brand.

In 1999, the San Francisco-based Skyy entered into a worldwide distribution deal with Gruppo Campari, makers of the popular bitter red Italian aperitif. This has enabled readier penetration of export markets than can normally be expected of a speciality brand. A bunch of five flavoured versions has been added, as has (in 2005) a premium-strength bottling, Skyy 90, made from winter wheat and with an alcohol content of 45%.

The packaging is highly distinctive. Eschewing the normal clear bottle, the producer opted for a deep cobalt-blue design, evocative of a clear night sky, with gold lettering.

Taste
Exemplary freshness and an almost ozone cleanness distinguish the nose of the principal bottling. On the palate, its absolute neutrality is reminiscent of an ultra-rectified Russian grain vodka. The spirit is impressively balanced, with no hard edges at all.

The flavoured variants are all bottled at 37.5% abv in the European markets and 35% in the United States. **Orange**, which is a blend of standard and

Made from	Wheat, filtered water
ABV	40%
Proof	80
Website	www.skyy.com
Origin	United States

blood oranges, has a sherbety, orange-crush kind of nose, but with suggestions of the peel of bitter orange on the palate. It is bravely quite pithy and bitter, and more of a grown-up product than many other orange vodkas. Mix it with Cointreau and freshly squeezed lemon juice for a good tangy cocktail.

Citrus is a blend of orange, lemon, lime, grapefruit and tangerine, and has something of the flavour of vodka mixed with fruit squash. **Berry** combines raspberry, blueberry, blackberry and redcurrant to give a pleasantly tangy nuance of just-picked hedgerow fruit. **Melon** is a juicy mixture of honeydew, canteloupe and watermelon, while **Vanilla**, discreet enough on the nose, opens out convincingly on the palate with authentic flavours of Madagascan vanilla pods.

SMIRNOFF

Synonymous with vodka the world over, Smirnoff leads its field in both market share and renown: only the white rum market leader, Bacardi, can match it. Whether in the liquor store or the cocktail bar, in the village pub or on an ocean liner, Smirnoff is ever-present. You may have graduated to investigating speciality brands that cost three or four times as much, or traded recklessly down to chain-store own-brand for a Friday night rowdy with friends, but this, undoubtedly, is where you started.

Fittingly, for a drink that is master of just about all it surveys, Smirnoff has a backstory worthy of Hollywood. It emerged from the ferment of twentieth-century political history and headed west in search of gold, effectively inventing the last major spirit category to arrive in the western cocktail cabinet until the advent of tequila.

The original brand was established during the high-water mark of Russian vodka production in the 1860s, when Piotr Smirnov opened a distillation plant in Moscow. The energetic competition of the previous half-century or so had led Russian vodka to a rarefied pitch of refinement, with producers from many different backgrounds vying to outdo each other for a slice of the market's top end. There was Smirnov vodka in crystal glasses at the Tsar's table, and it was supplied by appointment to many other aristocratic families; its satin softness entitling it to the kind of treatment previously accorded chiefly to imported wines.

Smirnov died in 1910, and his son Vladimir, born in 1875, inherited the business. Already an economic powerhouse, it continued to flourish until its annual production was a magisterial four million cases. It was one of the reference brands of imperial Russia, with a client list among the landed gentry that others could only envy. As such, it was eminently positioned to be engulfed by the red tide of 1917.

The October Revolution swept away the Tsarist excesses and it was also, perhaps surprisingly, driven by a prohibitionist fervour that uncannily echoed the legislative forces massing in the United States at the same period.

Above: Smirnov Vodka advertisement, 1911. In this pre-revolutionary period, the product came proudly garlanded with its imperial crests, denoting its Royal Appointment status.

Above: Smirnoff Vodka advertisement, 1953. By this time vodka was being promoted as a chic alternative martini base.

But where American prohibition was driven by salvationist zeal, Bolshevik hostility to alcohol was a social issue. Cheap vodka was the tool of oppression with which capitalism kept the workers stupefied when they were not creating its profits through their labour. Sober the masses up, Lenin reasoned, and you will unleash the creative energies needed to construct the first ever workers' state.

Smirnov's distillery was confiscated by the Bolshevik government, and production terminated. Smirnov himself escaped to join the counter-revolutionary White Army forces. Captured in a skirmish in 1919, he was imprisoned and sentenced summarily to death. For five nights running, he was told he would be shot the following morning as an enemy of the revolution. Nobody quite got round to the fateful task, and on the fifth day, a detachment of White forces stormed the prison and liberated the detainees.

Smirnov took the route out of Russia's maelstrom that Leon Trotsky would take a decade later, escaping to Turkey. The distillery rose again in Istanbul in 1920, rudimentarily equipped with apparatus, but richly endowed with the expertise of its founder. In 1924, he moved to Lwow (then in Poland, now Lviv, Ukraine), and altered the brand name spelling to the French variant of Russian name-endings, Smirnoff. Here, the seeds of its modern commercial success were sown. The following year, a subsidiary facility was established in Paris.

Many European consumers were introduced to vodka during this, the first great cocktail era of the twentieth century. There is a tiny pinch of vodka recipes in the *Savoy Cocktail Book* published in 1930, but it was clear that, whatever fringe connoisseurship the drink enjoyed, it wasn't seen as a natural mixing ingredient.

In 1933, as the result of a chance encounter in Paris, Smirnov sold the right to produce his vodka in North America to Rudolf Kunett, whose family had done business with the Smirnovs in the pre-revolutionary days in Moscow. Initially, it flopped, with barely enough revenue being generated to pay for the alcohol licences a post-prohibitionist US had reintroduced. A few years later, the rights were sold on to the Heublein company of Connecticut, whose then president, John Martin, was steeped in the ways of the American drinks market and recognized an untapped goldfield when he saw one.

When it came to strong liquor, what most Americans drank was their own corn whiskey. If consumers could be encouraged to see vodka, its distant kin as a grain spirit, as a form of lighter, purer 'white whiskey', as Martin styled it, the deluge would surely follow. That, in the period following the uneasy alliance with Moscow during the Second World War, was precisely what happened.

Vodka took its place in the pared-down cocktail culture of the 1950s. It made a fine Martini for those who had never quite discovered the taste for gin, as depicted in the advertisement on the facing page. To the suburban salary-man coming home from a day's breadwinning, it was a gentler recourse than the bourbon bottle. And it was mostly Smirnoff that he drank. In the years to come, it migrated back to European shores, and its modern ascendancy was secured.

Rival Russian products claiming to be the true Smirnoff have arisen and been legally dispatched in recent years. The brand is now part of Diageo, a gigantic international drinks corporation that extends from Irish Guinness to George Dickel Tennessee Whisky, via Gordon's gin and Captain Morgan rum.

The flagship Red Label bottling, distilled under licence in the UK and other territories, is one of the most familiar labels in the spirits business. It is accorded a rather higher level of care in manufacture than may be expected of a brand leader. Triple-distilled, the vodka is subjected to an eight-hour filtration process through activated carbon, during which it passes through the filtering system no fewer than ten times. All this is in pursuit of as near to a perfect neutrality of style as possible.

Taste

Smirnoff **Red Label**, historically known as No 21, has, not surprisingly, a very clean, plain nose, in the Russian manner. In the mouth, the spirit is gently sweet and some intriguing, discreet herbal tones emerge. There is perhaps a suggestion of freshly washed basil leaves, but the overall profile is impeccably neutral and refined, with no spirit catch on the finish.

Smirnoff **Blue Label**, or No 57, is treated to the same regime as the Red Label, but is bottled at the higher strength of 45% abv. Again, the nose is clean and dead neutral, the palate full of mountain-spring freshness. It tastes brisk, vigorous, even wholesome, with a gently simmering alcohol presence pushing gently through at the end.

The **Black Label**, No 55, is small-batch distilled in copper pot stills and filtered through silver birch charcoal for a premium vodka experience. Bottled at 40% abv, it has immediately more noticeable aromatic character, with herbal scents of basil and bitter leaves (radicchio), together with a hint of mint. The palate is full of attractive herbal notes, is hugely complex and rounded, and finishes with lovely caramel-soft spirit. This is a fine vodka to drink as it comes, straight from the freezer.

Smirnoff has proceeded boldly into the flavoured market. **Nordic**, a version of the No 21 bottled at 37.5% and flavoured with a mixture of wild berries, has a delicate electric-blue colour and a very gentle blueberry nose, supported by something distinctly more exotic and tropical, like passionfruit. Its flavours are light and subtle on the palate, presumably so as to keep it convivial with mixers, and it finishes on a dry, savoury note.

The flavour range includes **Black Cherry**, **Citrus**, **Cranberry**, **Green Apple**, **Lime**, **Orange**, **Passion Fruit**, **Raspberry**, **Strawberry**, **Vanilla** and **Watermelon**.

Made from	Grain, demineralized water
ABV	37.5%
Proof	75
Website	www.smirnoff.com
Origin	Russia

SNOW LEOPARD

Environmental concerns lie at the heart of many niche products in the present era, and here is a Polish vodka that aims to do something to protect the dwindling populations of one of central Asia's rarest wild mammals. Snow leopards live at the kinds of high altitudes that human beings once shunned, but with encroachment into their habitat and consequent decline in their food sources, as well as the receding of the snowline in the face of climate change, their numbers are shrinking. Fifteen per cent of the profits on sales of this vodka go to the Snow Leopard Trust.

It may seem a long way from the mountain ridges of Tajikistan to the Polmos distillery at Lublin, but as environmental campaigners point out, we all live in the one world. It is also a long way from Poland to Egypt, where the grain from which Snow Leopard vodka is made was first systematically cultivated. Spelt (*Triticum spelta*) is relatively rarely used today – other than as an animal feed – compared to its workhorse cousin, common wheat. It is highly nutritious, though, and has a longer pedigree as an agricultural crop. It fell foul of the first threshing machines in the late eighteenth century, which had difficulty penetrating the tough outer husk of the grains, and farmers in much of Europe simply stopped planting it.

Situated about 240 km (150 miles) south-east of Warsaw, the distillery at Lublin has been producing vodkas for the past century. Snow Leopard was launched in 2006. It is distilled four times, and blended with spring water from an on-site deep-water well.

The bottle, as you would expect, depicts the eponymous creature in all its spotted nobility against a bleak, frozen mountain landscape. The hard-shouldered cylindrical shape is offset by a slight waisting in the centre, making it easy to hold when pouring.

Taste
It has a very discreet, delicately grainy nose, with a slight suggestion of muesli. On entry to the palate, it is beautifully soft, with an amazingly gentle mouth-feel. There is nothing particularly exotic about the taste, but this

Made from	Spelt, deep-well water
ABV	40%
Proof	80
Website	www.snowleopardvodka.com
Origin	Poland

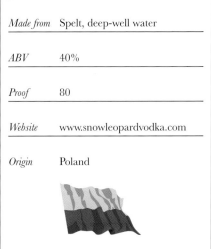

is nonetheless a powerfully attractive vodka, with a long, warm, silky finish.

Snow Leopard makes a fine vodka martini. Rinse the ice in dry vermouth, pour it away, then stir the vodka with the seasoned ice in a mixing jug. Strain into a cocktail glass and garnish with a twist of lime peel.

SNOW QUEEN

With the breakup of the Soviet Union at the beginning of the 1990s, a group of newly independent countries emerged. Many of these had been home to distilleries during the Soviet era, and the expertise that had been invested in them was put to use producing a new generation of vodkas.

Snow Queen is the premier vodka of Kazakhstan, a huge state now on the southern Russian border. It is very much an upmarket modern product, as is evident from the glacial maiden who adorns the bottles, and the raw materials and distillation procedures that combine to make it. The company boasts that no artificial ingredient comes near it.

It is made from organically grown wheat, blended with sand-filtered artesian spring water from the foothills of the snow-capped Tian Shan mountains in the south-east of the country, and the final filtration is done through birch charcoal sourced from sustainable Kazakh forests. The spirit receives five distillations in pursuit of the smooth-textured elegance of a niche vodka, and is rigorously tested at all stages of the process for the presence of any unwanted compounds.

An incurably romantic sensibility has been poured into the bottle design, which features a wind-swept, warlike monarch holding a staff, above the towering steeples of traditional Kazakh church architecture. The promotional literature is, perhaps inevitably, written in the style of one of the more bleakly haunting Hans Christian Andersen fairytales.

Taste
As suits the brand image, this is an immaculately clean vodka, fresh and ozone-pure on the nose, with a palate of astringent freshness. The spirit is soft, embracing and whistle-clean, very discreet and well-behaved given the absence of any notable flavour elements, and leading to a spotless, bracing finish.

This is a benchmark for the dead neutral but ultra-refined style of eastern vodka. It drinks beautifully if served snow-cold from the freezer in a classic vodka martini, but is a fine mixer with grapefruit juice or best lemonade.

Made from	Organic wheat, spring water
ABV	40%
Proof	80
Website	www.snowqueenvodka.com
Origin	Kazakhstan

SOBIESKI

The producers of Sobieski are most insistent on the historical origins of vodka lying in Poland, rather than Russia, in the 'early Middle Ages'. This product is named after one of the outstanding monarchs and military leaders in Polish history, Jan Sobieski, who reigned as King Jan III from 1674 until his death in 1696. Nor was he any mere hereditary monarch. Having repeatedly distinguished himself in battle, at a time when the Polish-Lithuanian commonwealth was under severe external threat and at the point of financial collapse, he was overwhelmingly elected to the throne by members of the Polish parliament. His most famous victory was seeing off invading Ottoman forces at the Battle of Vienna in 1683.

Sobieski vodka is one of those products that refuses to make a gratuitous show of itself. It doesn't claim multiple distillations, oddball ingredients or a bottle produced in the hothouse of a design consultancy. Its two principal ingredients are Polish rye, specifically the Dankowski Gold variety, and a source of pure spring water dating back to the Oligocene geological era (about 30 million years ago).

The bottle is unashamedly old-fashioned, with the Polish eagle embossed beneath the neck, and the brand name and label set in the national colours of red and white, incorporating a cartouche bearing an image of the king.

Taste
Sobieski has a beguiling, rounded aroma of rich cereal grains (hints of muesli). The palate is marked by a chalky-dry texture and a satisfyingly dense wholemeal taste. A fugitive hint of quinine is suggested on the finish, which is weighty and powerful. It tastes intriguingly stronger than it is, and yet without any extraneous spirit burn. A high-impact vodka, even the lower-strength bottling for the UK market (37.5% abv) lacks nothing in structure and concentration.

Sobieski Estate, with its heavy metallic top, is a single-varietal vodka made exclusively from the Dankowski Gold rye variety grown in Poland's Galicia region. It has a graceful delicacy on the nose, which belies the big, assertive

Made from	Rye, Oligocene spring water
ABV	40%
Proof	80
Website	www.vodkasobieski.com
Origin	Poland

palate, and the same dry graininess as the standard bottling rather than the sweetness of some other rye vodkas. There is alcohol emphasis on the finish (like the standard Sobieski, it's bottled at 40%), making for a powerful but flawlessly rounded spirit.

SOPLICA

Many of Poland's best-known quality vodkas are made from rye, which tends to give a richer-tasting spirit than a wheat vodka, but Soplica is based on a mix of the two grains. It is produced these days at a distillery in Oborniki in western Poland, but when production of the brand began, back in 1891, it was made at the nearby town of Gniezno, one of the centres of the nascent medieval Polish state in the tenth century.

This brand is named after the hero of the Polish national verse epic, *Pan Tadeusz* (1834) by Adam Mickiewicz. The story is set in the time of the partition of the Polish-Lithuanian kingdom by the Russians and others. In part, it's a Romeo and Juliet tale revolving around a romance between two lovers on opposite sides of a feudal familial divide, but it also recounts a successful uprising against the Russian occupiers in which Tadeusz Soplica emerges as the hero. It was first filmed in the silent era in 1928, and most recently by the great Polish director Andrzej Wajda in 1999.

The production process in a column still consists of four separate distillations, followed by rectification through activated charcoal. Although already derived from a pure source, the water used is subjected to its own filtration before being blended with the spirit.

Its revamped bottle design features a clear label with the red brand name out-lined in silver beneath an image of the sabre-wielding Soplica on horseback. A design of curved silver lines resembles sword slashes, and the shoulder of the bottle has grooves moulded into the glass to complete a martial design.

Taste

On the nose, Soplica is bracingly fresh, with the distinct tang of just-washed salad leaves. It strikes the palate with a positive, assertive flavour range and alcohol that doesn't hide its light under a bushel. Hints of aniseed enliven the finish, which is sharply defined, lively and complex.

This is a great vodka for using in the traditional Polish mix with apple juice. Use the best pressed apple juice you can find, and just a chunk or two of ice.

Made from	Rye, wheat, spring water
ABV	40%
Proof	80
Origin	Poland

STOLICHNAYA

Known the world over by its affectionate diminutive, Stoli, Stolichnaya is perhaps the pre-eminent quality Russian vodka. It has become synonymous with the Russian origins of distilled grain spirits, a heritage that is unhesitatingly celebrated by the brand's producers.

The name refers to the spirit's home in Moscow, since *stolitsa* is the Russian word for 'capital city'. It was first produced toward the end of the Tsarist era in 1901, at a state facility in Moscow specifically established to ensure a certain level of purity in the manufacture of the national drink. Production of Stolichnaya, which became the sole prerogative of the private SPI Group in 1997 after the disintegration of the Soviet Union, has lately been the subject of an energetic legal tussle. In 2002, a Moscow court ruled that use of the brand name should be restored to the Russian Ministry of Agriculture, but this was in turn contested by a ruling in the US Federal Courts in 2006 to the effect that SPI had the right to use of the brand name in export markets.

A blend of wheat and rye grains goes into the initial mash, which is distilled four times up to the standard spirit strength of around 96%, before being mixed with artesian water from the Kaliningrad region. The final filtration is a three-stage process that utilizes first granular quartz, then activated charcoal, and finally coarse cloth.

The label shows the name written in ornate gold script over a line drawing of a building that was once the Hotel Moskva (Moscow), an architectural hotchpotch built during the Stalinist 1930s and demolished in 2004. The label also wears its row of medals as ostentatiously as any commissar at a Red Army march past.

Stolichnaya is a multifarious product. As well as different grades and strengths of the neutral vodka (red-label, blue-label, Gold, Elit), there is a plethora of flavoured versions with eccentric but decipherable spellings including: **Blakberi**, **Blueberi**, **Citros** (lemon and lime), **Cranberi**, **Kafya**, **Ohranj**, **Peachik**, **Razberi**, **Strasberi** and **Vanil**.

Made from	Wheat and rye, artesian well water
ABV	40%
Proof	80
Website	int.stoli.com
Origin	Russia

Taste

The flagship **red-label** Stoli has the classic Russian dead-neutral, spanking-clean nose, and is also a textbook example of ultra-rectified Russian grain spirit on the palate, dense-textured but spotlessly clean, with a strong spirit finish. **Gold**, which comes confusingly with a black label and used to be known as Cristall, is even fuller-bodied, with gentle spicy notes of aniseed and pepper.

The **blue-label** bottling is more powerful in spirit, having 50% abv, with big, arresting, buttery richness. **Elit**, the ultra-refined version, which is bottled at 40% abv and undergoes a freezing filtration for that extra touch of driven-snow purity, is brisk and clean, and once again strikes the palate with the suggestion that what you are drinking is pure spirit and water and absolutely nothing else.

STUMBRAS

The Stumbras company, founded during the Tsarist era in 1906, is the pre-eminent distiller in what is now once again independent Lithuania. Its history is traced under another of its labels, Lithuanian Original (see page 132). Privatized in 2003, it entered its second century in pole position in Lithuania, producing a range of highly crafted and internationally recognized distilled spirits (vodka most famously, but also brandies, liqueurs and bitters).

The range bottled under the name of the distillery itself offers us a fascinating opportunity to taste pure vodkas made from each of the two principal grains, and also a zubrowka style, flavoured with bison grass.

Stumbras Centenary was launched to celebrate the company's first hundred years of operations. It is a wheat vodka, as is indicated not just by the image of a golden wheatfield under a clear blue sky on the inside back of the bottle, but also a whole ear of ripe wheat bobbing about in the drink. The vodka is made from carefully selected grain and purified water, and filtered through silver for final clarity.

Stumbras Rye Bread vodka bears a back-bottle image of slices of dark brown rye bread, and there is a handful of rye grains at the bottom of the bottle. Some of the organically grown rye is baked into bread, from which an extract is prepared and matured for over a month. Silver filtration is practised for this vodka too.

Taste
Stumbras **Centenary** has an intense, pleasantly medicinal nose with some aniseed and plenty of depth, followed up by a big, characterful palate with forthright spice notes (coriander, cloves). The spirit is powerful but impressively mellow, with a dry, savoury finish.

Stumbras **Rye Bread** vodka has a gorgeously inviting aroma of black bread and also suggests richer, deeper notes of treacle glazes and ginger. The palate is altogether fabulous, opulent in flavour like gingerbread or French *pain*

Made from	Various grains, filtered water
ABV	40%
Proof	80
Website	www.stumbras.eu
Origin	Lithuania

d'épice, intensely savoury, appetizing and nutritious in character (it tastes as though it's packed with B vitamins), with a toasty, caraway-seed finish and massive complexity. A triumph of the distiller's art.

For the **Buffalo Grass** bottling, see Zubrówka, page 212.

SVEDKA

One glance at its website will confirm that Svedka, originally launched in 1998, is a concept vodka par excellence. It styles itself as having been voted the Number One vodka of the year 2033, so its manufacturers are clearly happy to be patient for it to receive its due recognition, and users of the site are invited to interact with a well-endowed Fembot, who may eventually be elected President of the United States.

Beneath all the riotous image-making is a serious product. It is produced in Sweden from homegrown wheat and crystal-clear spring water, with around 7 kg (3 pounds) of the grain being required for each 70cl bottle. While the recipe itself harks back centuries, we are told, the technology is bang up to date. Five distillations in a column still help to round out the spirit.

The Svedka brand was acquired by the giant Constellation Brands drinks group in 2007, but its quirkily individualistic image remains unaffected. At the time of writing, it is the second biggest Swedish vodka brand on the international market.

The bottle design is defiantly minimal, with bold blue lettering on clear glass above a small Swedish flag.

Taste
Clinical neutrality is the name of the game for the plain vodka. The palate is fresh and crisp, as sheer as brushed steel in its impact, and spotlessly clean in the Russian style. Its alcohol content is assertive but enticingly contoured, building up to a big, muscular finish. It's an ideal vodka for blending with quality fruit juices.

A portfolio of four natural flavours is offered. **Citron** contains California lemons and Mexican limes; **Clementine** is made with fruit from Sicily and Calabria in southern Italy; a pure fruit essence is subjected to a six-fold concentration process for the **Raspberry**; and **Vanilla** uses whole vanilla beans. Available in the North American market, these are bottled at 35% abv, just below the minimum strength for vodka within the European Union.

Made from	Wheat, spring water
ABV	40%
Proof	80
Website	www.svedka.com
Origin	Sweden

SVENSK

The story of Svensk is a tribute to the indomitable Scandinavian spirit. It was conceived and launched in 1996, soon after Sweden's accession to the European Union, by a pair of entrepreneurs, Michael Lindberg and Mikael Andersson.

Since the early years of the twentieth century, spirits production had been a state monopoly in Sweden, much as it was in the former communist countries, but with EU membership came greater commercial freedom. Lindberg and Andersson were the first private producers of distilled spirits in the country since 1917. With that unique selling point, the brand enjoyed initial success, but quickly faltered in the rapaciously competitive market for such products. It was rescued from bankruptcy and near-certain extinction as a brand by a wine export company, Fondberg, in late 2001. And so Svensk lives to fight another day.

The happy ending was richly deserved. This is in every sense a carefully crafted product, made from locally grown wheat, the grain distillate blended with ice-cold water from Lake Vättern, a long, narrow lake in the centre of southern Sweden, the second largest in the country and one of the most extensive stretches of fresh water in the world. The distillery also doubles as a recycling plant for seizures of illegal spirits, which are transformed into public transport fuel for the residents of the town of Linköping, to the east of Lake Vättern.

A tall, beautifully understated bottle shows the brand name in white against a blue neckband, with the name reflected beneath as though in the surface of the icy lake.

Taste

From the first sniff, Svensk turns on the charm. It has a head-turning aromatic profile that plays on green fruits such as melon and guava, but also has a little of the character of freshly washed green beans. The sharply defined fruity impact continues on the palate, with kiwi and musky melon notes, all brought into focus with crisp but not aggressive spirit. That, plus

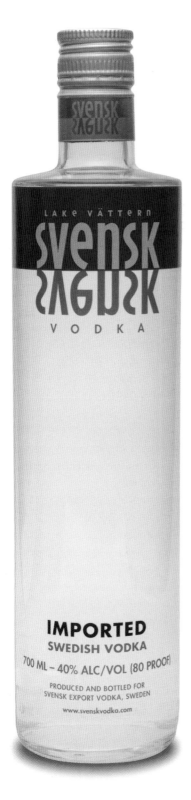

Made from	Wheat, lake water
ABV	40%
Proof	80
Website	www.svenskvodka.com
Origin	Sweden

a long, complex finish, makes it a very interesting neat shot, but also fits it to marry well with a variety of fruit juices and other flavours.

An array of four flavour variants creates a versatile range. **Lemon** and **Wild Strawberry** led the charge, and were followed by **Vanilla** and **Apple**. And to complete the picture, there is a Svensk gin.

TOVARITCH!

Here we have one of those Russian vodkas that nostalgically celebrates the Soviet era. Unexpectedly, it is the creation of an Italian entrepreneur, Eugenio Litta, established in 1999 and produced at a distillery in Lytkarino, just outside Moscow.

Tovaritch (or *tovarich*, in the more usual English transliteration) is the Russian for 'comrade'. It is also the title of a once-popular comic play, written in 1933 by French dramatist Jacques Deval, which tells the tale of two members of the Russian nobility who flee to Paris from the Bolshevik Revolution, with the Tsar's crown jewels in safekeeping. They disguise themselves as commoners and get jobs in domestic service, but are rumbled when a visiting Soviet dignitary recognizes them. The piece was filmed by Warner Brothers in 1937, with Claudette Colbert and Charles Boyer in the lead roles, and Basil Rathbone as Commissar Gorotchenko.

The vodka is made in the sparkling-clean Russian style from quality grain. It is distilled five times and then subjected to a triple rectification through birch charcoal and blended with artesian spring water.

Inspiration for the bottle design is drawn from the Soviet agitprop style of the 1920s, as typified by the graphic works of the poet and playwright Vladimir Mayakovsky (1893–1930). A Russian worker poses heroically, gesturing toward the future against the rising sun of communism. This was a graphic idiom known as Komfut (Communist Futurism), and one that would swiftly meet its doom, as indeed did Mayakovsky himself, in the stifling atmosphere of cultural orthodoxy that held sway under Stalin.

Taste
There is a faint touch of something herbal (fresh basil) about the nose, with perhaps a breath of musky spice (coriander seed). On the palate, this is a weighty vodka, with dense, concentrated texture, and a less neutral style than other Russian vodkas. It tastes interestingly spicy, grainy and complex, and finishes assertively on those notes – very much a 'neat' style of vodka, best enjoyed on its own, or with ice and a twist.

Made from	Wheat, spring water
ABV	40%
Proof	80
Website	www.tovaritch.com
Origin	Russia

ULTIMAT

An indisputably upmarket product, as its name announces, Ultimat aims for the best of all worlds, using potatoes and two types of grain in different proportions to achieve an ultimately harmonious and complex spirit. The intention is that each of the three components brings something distinctive to the flavour of the final product – potato for traditional Polish richness, rye for its grainy complexity and wheat for textural smoothness. It is the only vodka in the world that combines all three.

It is produced by the makers of the premium tequila brand, Patrón. A state-of-the-art distillation procedure, known as hydro-selection, is used, and the vodka is blended with artesian well water and ceramic-filtered. To emphasize the hands-on nature of the production, filtration takes place against candle-light – just as though it were a venerable old wine that was being decanted.

Ultimat comes in one of the more eye-catching bottles on the market, a two-toned cobalt-blue and clear crystal decanter with a large crystal-headed cork stopper. Each bottle is hand-blown over 24 hours, the final touch being a little bubble in the base.

Taste
The vodka is assertively rich on the nose, even slightly earthy, and the palate is powerful and weighty, with the flavour of potato baking in the oven, just at the point where the skin has begun to singe, noticeable among its array of flavours. It finishes sweet and rich, with forthright but composed alcohol.

A crowd-pleasing flavour variant, **Chocolate Vanilla**, has been launched in a white bottle. Combining the two ingredients in admirable balance, I'm told it makes a luxurious addition to a mug of late-night cocoa. There is also a **Black Cherry** version.

Made from	Potatoes, wheat and rye, demineralized artesian water
ABV	40%
Proof	80
Website	www.ultimatvodka.com
Origin	Poland

U'LUVKA

A brand with a head-turning name, U'Luvka has a backstory to match. It was conceived in 2005 in commemoration of the work of Michal Sedziwój (1566–1636). Better known as Michael Sendivogius, he was a chemist, doctor and practitioner of alchemy, who found favour with the royal courts of Poland and Bohemia. The roots of distillation in Europe were closely bound up with alchemy, as its exponents sought to extract the essence or spirit of fermented brews by the application of heat.

When Sedziwój arrived at the court of King Sigismund III in Kraków around 1600, he was extravagantly feted. The king provided him with his own experimental laboratory on the premises (still preserved today at Wawel Castle), and one of his tasks was to come up with a purer formula for the distilled clear spirit with which members of the court were saturated more or less daily. Legend has it that it was one of Sedziwój's potions that helped the king see off a life-threatening illness at the age of 40, and live on for another 25 years.

U'Luvka's globetrotting British founder, Mark Holmes, touched by the long, strong tradition of vodka-based domestic hospitality in Poland, pursued a series of sedulous researches there to unearth old recipes and techniques. His vodka comprises a three-way grain mix of rye, wheat and barley, the brew distilled in classic small batches, blended with pure water from deep-lying wells. To retain some of the natural distillation flavours, U'Luvka is restricted to three distillations: the aim is not ultra-refined neutrality.

When it comes to designer packaging, U'Luvka rewrites the book. Its teardrop-shaped body and sinuously wavy neck, topped with a cork stopper, makes it look like a particularly opulent *parfum*, and it has attracted a lot of interest on retail shelves from women shoppers in a section of the drinks store – premium spirits – that is traditionally a male haunt.

Taste

Aromatically discreet, with perhaps a distant suggestion of caraway, it opens out into richly savoury notes on the palate. The spirit is unapologetically

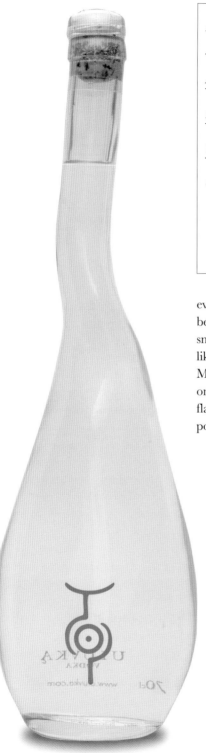

Made from	Rye, wheat and barley, deep-well water
ABV	40%
Proof	80
Website	www.uluvka.com
Origin	Poland

evident, as befits a vodka that hasn't been over-rectified. To me, it's a smart choice with something spicy like ginger ale for a classic Moscow Mule (*pace* its Polish origins), or one of the more assertively flavoured juices, like cranberry or pomegranate.

UTKINS UK5

More than any other spirit, vodka lends itself to today's concern with green and environmental issues. It is, after all, intended to be as pure as the driven snow in taste and appearance, and doesn't involve procedures such as aging in barrels. It seems only natural, then, for the market to be open to an organic vodka.

Made in Surrey, southern England, and launched in 2001, UK5 is based on grain that hasn't been sprayed with chemical pesticides or fungicides (and which is thereby claimed to retain a denser cell structure and higher natural sugars, producing a more characterful vodka), blended with the purest water. Its manufacturers want you to enjoy the healthy sporting life, and they promote activities such as skiing and kite-surfing.

The rye grain used is grown on a certified organic farm in Germany. The spirit is made in what are claimed to be the two smallest working stills in London, nicknamed Tom Thumb and Thumbelina. Uniquely, no filtration is carried out, not because filtration itself is a bad thing, but because the spirit isn't deemed to need it, being so innocent of impurities in the first place. That means that a lot of the naturally rich by-products of distillation remain in the vodka, contributing to its overall complexity. Technically speaking, it is comparatively high in ethyl acetate, which makes for a pleasingly soft texture in the mouth.

There is nothing overly elaborate about the bottle design, as one would expect from a product informed by green thinking. The name appears in bold, stencil-style lettering on a clear bottle, with pride of place given to the badge of the Prince of Wales, well known for his support of organic produce.

Taste
Like all rye vodkas, UK5 has an assertively grainy nose. You may be reminded of muesli, or the toasted grains in a good breakfast cereal. This note continues on the crisp, grainy palate. The alcohol note is perhaps a little edgier than the overall softness of the spirit might lead you to expect, but that complex, grainy depth of flavour easily carries it. With its exemplary level of

Made from	Organic rye, spring water
ABV	40%
Proof	80
Website	www.uk5.org
Origin	UK (England)

purity, this vodka is crying out to be the base of a therapeutic morning-after Bloody Mary, but it is a good general mixer too. Hearteningly for an organic product, its retail price has been kept within sensible bounds.

VAN GOGH

The most innovative vodka of the Netherlands is named after the troubled genius of nineteenth-century Dutch art, extravagant homage to whom is paid in a series of eye-catching bottle designs. Although a neutral vodka is produced (as well as a gin), it's fair to say that the chief selling point of Van Gogh is its extensive flavour range – 17 at the time of writing, more than any other single brand can boast. They are aimed squarely at the international cocktail circuit.

The vodkas are made at the Royal Dirkzwager plant at Schiedam near Rotterdam in the Netherlands, at which distilling was established in the 1880s during Van Gogh's lifetime. This brand, launched in 2000, is the product of a complex triple distillation process, in which the first two stages take place in a column still, and the final one in a copper pot still. A tripartite combination of wheat, corn and barley forms the basis of the spirit.

The round-shouldered cylindrical bottle has a window effect in the centre, through which a gallery of Van Gogh-style images can be seen, including a self-portrait for the neutral bottling and one of the famous *Sunflowers* series of 1888.

Taste
The aromatic impact of the neutral vodka is big and assertive, with woody and grainy notes in abundance. On the palate, it is pleasantly soft, with overtones of coffee in a nicely rounded mouth-feel that speaks of careful filtration.

Not only has Van Gogh broken new ground with its prolific flavour range, but some of the vodkas are coloured too. **Acai-Blueberry** is a delicate mauve, with overtones of Parma violet in the taste and a fairly heavy, syrupy palate. **Double Espresso,** one of the most successful flavours, is deep tawny in colour and has an appealingly rich mocha coffee aroma and flavour, with the discreet alcohol note you expect to find in an Irish coffee (together with the caffeine). There is also an **Espresso** version with the coffee flavour, but no colour and no caffeine.

Made from	Wheat, corn and barley
ABV	40%
Proof	80
Website	www.vangoghvodka.com
Origin	Netherlands

The list goes on with **Pineapple**, **Coconut**, **Dutch Chocolate**, **Wild Appel**, **Pomegranate** (also coloured), **Banana**, **Vanilla**, **Raspberry**, **Oranje**, **Citroen**, **Melon**, **Mango**, **Black Cherry** and **Mojito Mint**. These are all bottled at the lower strength of 35% abv.

VILLA LOBOS

If you could use some exotic booze, you needn't look too much further than Villa Lobos, Mexico's entry in the vodka stakes. Made by the Licores Veracruz distillery, near the port of the same name, Villa Lobos (Sin Rival – Unrivalled – to give it its domestic brand name) is certainly a head-turner.

The Caribbean port of Veracruz was once a hotbed of piracy, which explains why it is overlooked by the imposing fifteenth-century prison fortress of San Juan de Ulúa.

Mexico has always had a strong, proud tradition of ardent spirits production, from the agave spirits, mezcal and tequila, to the country's own versions of grape brandy. Vodka seems a natural extension of this repertoire, but you can bet that it will have its own highly distinctive regional characteristics.

Villa Lobos is a blend of three cereal grains: corn, wheat and barley. The water used is derived from artesian sources that are filled from the melted snows of Mexico's highest active volcano, El Pico de Orizaba, which is snow-capped even in the broiling heat of the Mexican summer. The vodka is distilled an impressive five times, and the principal version also contains a worm for good measure.

The 'worm' (actually the larva of the night butterfly, *Cossus redtembachi*) is the same creature that lurks in the bottom of your bottle of mezcal. Indigenous folk belief has long attributed to it the power to bring out your inner hero, and it was traditionally eaten in a preparatory ritual before battle.

On the label, a gun-toting Mexican *bandito* in his sombrero lounges menacingly in what looks like a window, keeping a beady eye on us while we nibble nonchalantly on some tacos and sip a glass of Villa Lobos.

Taste
The agave worm bottling has a distant suggestion of mezcal on the nose. It has a waxy aromatic profile, and is similarly agave-like on the palate. It's also richly grainy and savoury, distinctly unusual, and the kind of drink of which

Made from	Corn, wheat and barley, volcanic meltwater
ABV	45%
Proof	90
Website	www.licoresveracruz.com
Origin	Mexico

a little – served very cold – would go a long way, especially given its higher-than-average alcohol content. Try it in a cocktail mix with equal parts Kahlúa (the Mexican coffee liqueur) and double cream.

There is also an over-strength bottling, **Platinum**, at 55% abv. This too is made from the same three grains and is distilled five times, but doesn't contain the worm. It has a strong antiseptic nose, the same delicately tequila-like backnote, but in a noticeably more refined style than its stablemate. That said, its powerful hit of alcohol emerges in full muscular force on the finish.

VLADIVAR

Vladivar has rather come up in the world, both literally and in terms of its image. Its production has moved northward from Lancashire in the north of England to Scotland, and it has made serious attempts to shake off the slight comedy image it acquired in the 1980s. The latter derived from an advertising campaign that played on the faintly amusing idea of vodka – with all its proud Slavic history – being made somewhere as prosaic-sounding as Warrington. To a whole generation it was, in the ham accent of the voiceover, 'Vladivar Vodka from Varrington'.

The Warrington connection is explained by its once having been a brand of the Lancashire brewer, Greenall Whitley, which sold the brand to Scotch whisky distillers Whyte & Mackay in 1990. It is gradually being repositioned as a more upscale product, with assertive modern packaging and a big advertising spend.

The vodka is a pure grain product that is subjected to the full kid-glove treatment of three distillations and filtration through charcoal for satiny texture and purity of flavour. Its production is overseen by a third-generation master distiller.

After various redesigns, the producers have settled on a clean, ice-blue label with a logo that features the double-headed eagle of somewhere much further east than Scotland, and a paragraph of descriptive text.

Taste

The nose is exceptionally clean, almost entirely neutral but with just the faintest tinge of aniseed. In the mouth, it has expansive, rounded texture, with just a little edge to the spirit, but the overall impression is of a brisk, clean vodka that's ideal for mixing. I picked up a fugitive hint of juniper on the finish, which suggests it would make a useful base for a thoroughly refreshing vodka-and-tonic.

Made from	Grain
ABV	37.5%
Proof	75
Website	www.vladivar.com
Origin	UK (Scotland)

TRIPLE DISTILLED

Vladivar

VODKA

Vladivar is a clean smooth vodka with a sophisticated flavour. Vladivar maintains a tradition of distilling excellence overseen by our third generation master distiller and is made from 100% pure grain, triple distilled and charcoal filtered.

70cl   37.5%vol

WHITE MISCHIEF

Is there any part of the alcohol-producing world left that isn't now making a vodka? India's runners in the international stakes are Romanov (see page 160) and this 'ultra-pure vodka', both owned and distributed by the giant UB Group, which also owns Sweden's Pinky (see page 146).

The Indian vodkas' original parent company, Shaw Wallace, founded in 1886, was a multi-disciplinary enterprise that imported the first motor cars into India, as well as being the Marconi wireless telegraph company's first agent in the country. Shaw Wallace was acquired by UB, complete with its extensive portfolio of drinks brands, in 2005. The UB portfolio today embraces whisky, brandy and rum, produced at 15 distilleries spread all over the country. There is also a White Mischief gin, in Ultra-Pure and London Lime versions.

Launched in 1996, White Mischief vodka has seen a well-nigh meteoric rise to commercial prominence, and is now the national market leader among those Indians who consume alcohol. It enjoys a nearly 50% share at the time of writing, principally in the Western Zone and Eastern Region sectors of the Indian market. Positioned as a premium product, it is based on triple-distilled spirit that is carbon-filtered to attain competitive levels of purity and smoothness of flavour. In 2007, it was announced that the brand ambassador for White Mischief would be Zayed Khan, the film actor whose credits include *Rocky: The Rebel* (2006) and *Cash* (2007).

The frosted bottle represents the fun-loving approach of the name, with the logo spelled out in bold red and blue.

Taste
The nose is clinically clean, not dissimilar to the Russian idiom, and then the higher-than-average spirit content comes roaring through. On the palate, it has a dry, chalky and grainy character, with quite close-knit texture and a massive, no-nonsense alcohol smoulder on the finish, reminiscent – you might say – of India's highly spiced cuisine.

Made from	Mixed grains, demineralized water
ABV	42.8%
Proof	85.6
Website	www.unitedspirits.in
Origin	India

WISNIOWKA

If lemon-flavoured vodkas from eastern Europe may not be quite what we expect from a cold northerly climate, cherry vodkas are much more likely candidates. Cherry trees were cultivated in Poland alongside apples, pears and plums from early medieval times. Their fruits were eaten fresh in the summer season, from July onwards, and then preserved in sugar syrup or honey for eating throughout the lean times of year. It was not unknown for abundant crops to keep a reasonably well-to-do family going through until next year's blossom was on the trees.

The *Domostroi*, a digest of Polish and Russian household management from the sixteenth and seventeenth centuries, advises readers to keep stocks of cherries stewed in syrup (a kind of compote) as a standby. Surpluses of cherries, raspberries and cranberries could also be boiled down to a concentrated fruit juice and stored through the winter, either to be drunk straight or used as an additive to jolly up the flavour of light beer or mead.

As well as various types of sweet cherry liqueur (similar to the cherry brandy of western Europe), Poland rejoices in *wisniówka*, one of the world's very greatest fruit-flavoured spirits. Made from quality grain spirit, the drink is flavoured with an infusion of different varieties of whole cherry – both sour and sweet – together with a further addition of some of the juice.

Taste

This version is made by Polmos Jozefow. The fruit infusions lend the drink a deep reddish-tawny colour. It has a nose reminiscent of cherries stewed in syrup, with slightly pruny notes mixed in, backed up by a delicately singed woody note, supported on masses of luscious alcohol. In the mouth, it is immediately apparent that this is a much more adult product than the flavoured fun drinks of today. Its flavour is gently sweet, medicinally tinged but also profoundly fruity, delicious and hugely complex, leading to a finish on which the spirit is perfectly integrated with the fruit flavours, like the best cask-aged fruit brandy. Trails of almond (from the cherry stones) and honey appear in the aftertaste.

Made from	Wheat, spring water
ABV	40%
Proof	80
Origin	Poland

To me, *wisniówka* is never going to taste better than when taken absolutely straight, at room temperature, as a mellower, fruitier alternative to a traditional barrel-aged digestif such as cognac or malt whisky. That said, it mixes sublimely with lemonade, and makes a very handsome component, along with lemon juice and soda, in a gin-based Singapore Sling.

WOKKA

Here is a recherché product if ever there was. Produced by a British distilling company, it is a blend of grain vodka with Japanese sake – distilled wheat spirit with fermented rice wine. The proportions are 80% vodka to 20% sake, and there is an infusion of exotic Asian fruits for good measure.

The manufacturing process is highly upscale, with micro-managed triple distillation in single batches in a pot still for the vodka base, after which the imported sake is manually blended in. It was launched in Miami in 2005, originally under the name of Wokka Saki, and is considered quite a hit as a partner to traditional sushi.

A bewitching natural phenomenon inspired the brand. Each winter, between January and March, the lower foothills of the Asahi mountains on Honshu (Japan's principal island) are buffeted by freezing westerly winds sweeping in from the Siberian plains of Russia and churning up icy vapour off the Sea of Japan. Gigantic coniferous trees on the slopes of Mount Zao bear the brunt of this onslaught, and are magically transformed into ice-bound creatures known to the Japanese people as *juhyo*, or 'snow monsters'. An annual Snow Monster Festival is held to celebrate their return.

Wokka is thus an East-meets-West conception, a marriage of the 'two noble cultures' of Russian vodka and Japanese rice wine, as symbolized by the impact of a western wind on the eastern landscape. It comes in a squat bottle of frosted glass, with a rough-edged paper label explaining the idea.

Taste
A pleasant, lightly fruity nose suggesting tropical fruits such as passionfruit, with maybe a little mango, opens up to a rounded, scented, vaguely floral palate that is full of charm. This is a highly perfumed product with a fairly prolonged, quite piercing aftertaste, but one that mixes improbably well, although it's also quite interesting on its own in small doses.

Among other cocktail ideas, the manufacturers propose Oriental Kiwi, a mix of five parts Wokka to two parts watermelon syrup and one part ginger and

Made from	Wheat, Japanese sake, Asian fruit
ABV	40%
Proof	80
Website	www.wokkasaki.com
Origin	UK (England)

lemongrass cordial. Crush a whole sliced kiwifruit into these ingredients, then shake with ice and strain into a tumbler of crushed ice, garnishing with a couple of slices of kiwi.

TRIPLE DISTILLATION
MICRO DISTILLED

WOKKA
SAKi™
VODKA

WITH A BLEND OF JAPANESE SAKE AND
A SUBTLE ESSENCE OF ASIAN FRUIT

*Inspired by the
snow monsters of Mt. Zao*

70cl e   40% vol

WINNER DOUBLE GOLD MEDALS
SAN FRANCISCO SPIRITS COMPETITION 2003, 2004 & 2005

WYBOROWA

Among the traditional old Polish brands of quality vodka, Wyborowa is one of the most internationally recognized. Its name means 'exquisite' in Polish, and its reputation for connoisseurial smoothness and opulence dates back nearly two centuries.

It was a product of the technological refinements that vodka began to undergo in the nineteenth century, but was in the vanguard even then. Established in 1823 at a distillery in Poznan owned by a wealthy entrepreneur, Hartwig Kantorowicz, Wyborowa had already made a stellar reputation for itself within Poland before it began to be exported in the 1860s. Having won a tasting competition at a time when the development of spirits brands was still in its commercial infancy, it eventually became, in 1927, the world's first trademarked vodka brand.

Wyborowa had become such a byword for quality by the time of vodka's first great wave of popularity in the west in the 1950s and '60s that, at one point, it accounted for over half of all the vodka imported into the UK. With the period of financial uncertainty in the 1990s that followed the collapse of the communist bloc, Wyborowa was acquired by the international drinks giant, Pernod Ricard.

It is made purely from rye, the grain that produces the richest and most complex of vodkas, and undergoes a triple distillation for satiny texture and purity. There is now also an ultra-refined version, which has been given the English name Exquisite, and comes in a bottle designed by the renowned American architect, Frank Gehry, designer of the titanium-clad Guggenheim Museum in Bilbao, Spain. It is produced in small batches at a single distillery at Turew in western Poland.

The traditional bottling still retains its glacially elegant packaging with dark blue lettering. Gehry's design for the Exquisite consists of a tall, narrow bottle twisted out of true, beneath a solid clear top like the head of a designer bath tap.

Made from	Rye, spring water
ABV	40%
Proof	80
Website	www.wodka.com
Origin	Poland

Taste

Wyborowa has a clean, neutral nose with a faint medicinal hint, and rounded, deeply rich rye texture in the mouth. The spirit is nicely integrated with the luxurious grainy flavours. **Exquisite** has a more powerful spirit aroma (although the strength is the same at 40%), but is infused with characteristic rye-vodka layers of chocolaty lushness on the palate. The impression left on the finish is all weighty authority – definitely one for appreciating neat.

Among the brand's burgeoning roll-call of flavour variants are: **Almond**, **Rose**, **Pear**, **Apple**, **Lemon**, **Melon**, **Orange**, **Pineapple**, **Peach**, **Pepper**, and a **Goldwasser** version full of gold sprinkles.

ZUBROWKA

A generic class of Polish vodkas is aromatized by the addition of bison grass. Known as *zubrówka*, or bison-grass vodka in English, it harks back to the very early days of distillation, when additions of herbal or botanical ingredients were often the best resort for masking the less-than-appealing character of unrectified spirit.

Bison grass (*Anthoxanthum nitens*) is an aromatic graminiferous herb that grows throughout the northern hemisphere, and goes by a number of alternative names in English, including sweet grass, holy grass and buffalo grass. It gains its animal associations from the beasts that roam in its habitat – in Poland's case, the dwindling herds of wild bison that inhabit the eastern forests of Białowieza, where the grass grows in clumps in the clearings. (Contrary to popular belief, the bison do not actually feed on it.)

The chief aromatic compound in bison grass is coumarin, also present in the tonka bean, that staple dessert ingredient on trendsetting restaurant menus of recent years. Used in perfumes and herbal medicines as well as spirit production, its characteristic scent is that of new-mown hay, shown at its best when the grass is harvested in the early summer months and left to dry.

In the distillation process, the rye vodka is passed through bundles of dried grass during condensation, when the spirit is vaporized and before it has returned to the liquid state. That usually gives the vodka a very gentle greenish tinge, and it is traditional to immerse a single blade of the grass in each bottle.

Labels generally depict the bison in all its shaggy nobility, either, as with Grasovka, staring out from clumps of its namesake grass, or else in regal profile, as with Zubrówka.

Taste
These vodkas are full of strange apothecarial scents that are at once fresh, grassy and intensely herbal. **Grasovka** has an appealingly medicinal character, with touches of cumin emerging on a palate that has an almost Chartreuse-like complexity, with a cutting edge of spirit at the end.

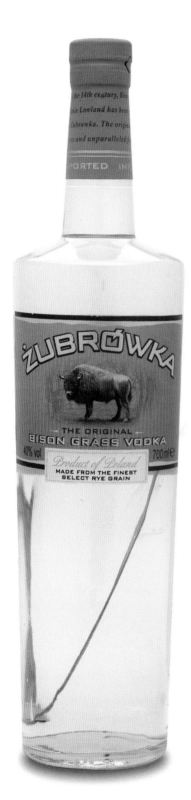

Made from	Rye, bison grass
ABV	40%
Proof	80
Origin	Poland

Zubrowka Bison Grass Vodka, from Poland's Polmos Bialystok distillery, is a very delicate greenish-yellow, hauntingly scented, with farmyardy notes emerging through the herbal tones, and something minty too. Indeed, there is a very definite minty tinge running through the palate, with menthol and caraway on the finish, supported by assertive spirit.

The **Stumbras** distillery in Lithuania (see page 132) has its own version, labelled **Buffalo Grass**, with an image of the grass growing in a forest clearing on the inside back of the bottle. It is lighter than the others, the woodruff and camomile hints emerging subtly on the palate, and with a gently spirited finish.

Bison grass vodkas are traditionally drunk neat and unchilled, or else mixed with apple juice, which blends beautifully with the herbal tones in the flavour.

Part 3
Vodka cocktails

Introduction to cocktails

It has never been possible to pinpoint the origin of the cocktail with much accuracy, but the term was already in use in the United States at the very beginning of the nineteenth century. The ancestors of the cocktail were the mixed drinks favoured in the social clubs, bars and racecourses of the fledgling Republic; initially they were not much more than a new way of dressing up traditional spirits such as whisky, brandy and rum with admixtures of water, lemon juice, mint or egg. An important early sourcebook is Jerry Thomas's *The Bar-Tender's Guide*, or *How To Mix Drinks* (1862).

The first and grandest international cocktail era, and the one that has in some sense provided the model for all subsequent ones, was the one that arose during what became known as the Jazz Age, a period of carefree licentiousness sandwiched between the twin disasters of the First World War and the Depression. This was also the precise period when alcohol Prohibition was in full sway in the United States, and the impetus behind many of the mixtures was simply the need to find resourceful ways of masking the ghastly flavour of bootleg, home-distilled liquor.

Cocktails faded from the scene during the worldwide emergencies of the 1930s and 1940s, and looked to have disappeared altogether – give or take the odd martini or Bloody Mary – by the post-war era. When the sun-and-sand antics of the international jet set began to become common property in the 1970s, though, cocktails (always an expensive way of drinking) began to stage a comeback, and the 1980s, which saw cocktail bars opening all over Europe, sealed it.

Equip yourself with sets of three types of glass – the martini glass, a tall glass for long drinks and a wide-mouthed tumbler – and as many of the alcohol ingredients in the following pages as you care to lay your hands on. Despite the acrobatics of Tom Cruise in that dreadful movie, cocktail-making doesn't require a showman's skill. Over-garnishing is out these days, and juggling with glasses belongs in the circus. There is really only one iron rule: never run out of ice.

• measurements are given in both ml and ounces.
• a standard measure is 25 ml in Europe and 1 ounce in the United States.

Neutral vodkas

SCREWDRIVER

First off, why Screwdriver? The story goes that when vodka first began to be popular in the United States in the 1950s, it was very much a blue-collar drink. Workers on oil rigs added orange crush to their vodka and, lacking for anything more delicate to hand, used their screwdrivers to stir the drink. Whatever the truth or otherwise of this story, the name became a useful hook in the 1980s for drinks to be given names that referenced sex (Slow Comfortable Screw, etc) with as little delicacy as those oil workers' improvized swizzle-sticks displayed.

50 ml/2 ounces plain vodka
freshly squeezed orange juice to
top up

The Screwdriver, be it noted, is just a vodka-and-orange; when it was served to Sir Winston and Lady Churchill at Eisenhower's White House in the 1950s, it aroused an unimpressed harrumph from the British premier. In the early days, the sour edge of pure orange juice was thought needful of being tempered with a spoonful of sugar, but not even teenagers bother with that now.

Pour the vodka over ice cubes in a tumbler and top with as much orange juice as you like – enough to soften the alcohol edge of the spirit. Garnish with a couple of half-slices of orange.

VODKA MARTINI

The original dry martini is a generous shot of icy gin with the merest moistening of dry vermouth, a great early-evening unwinder for those who are rather partial to gin. This version basically came about for those who are not.

Also known as the Vodkatini, it was popularized by the James Bond novels, in which 007 famously specifies that the drink should be 'shaken, not stirred', and made with vodka as well as gin.

50 ml/2 ounces plain vodka
a few drops of dry vermouth
(Noilly Prat is good)

At its first appearance, in 'Casino Royale' (1953), Bond stipulates the ingredients as three measures of Gordon's gin to one of vodka and a half-measure of Kina Lillet (a dry, wine-based herbal aperitif). By the time this bespoke recipe made it to the film screenplays, the gin had disappeared, but the instruction to shake remained. Shaking with ice clouds the drink, making it look all the frostier, whereas stirring leaves it clear. You decide.

Shake or stir the vodka with ice (stirring can afford to be a languid, two-minute process, shaking is for those in a hurry). Moisten a chilled martini glass by rolling a few drops of vermouth around it, pour it out and add the prepared vodka. Garnish to taste with a stuffed green cocktail olive (on a stick if you prefer), or a twist of lemon dangling in the drink.

MOSCOW MULE

The Moscow Mule dates from the very beginning of vodka's career in the West in the 1940s. It was the creation of John Martin of Heublein, the American company that had bought the rights to Smirnoff vodka, and a Los Angeles barman, Jack Morgan. Martin needed a selling angle for the new spirit, and was pondering over what to suggest to the public as a good mixer,

50 ml/2 ounces plain vodka
juice of a lime
ginger beer or ginger ale to top up

when Morgan happened to mention that he had landed himself with a job-lot quantity of ginger beer. The mixture was tried and cautiously approved, but found to need a dash of something else to sharpen it. A squeeze of lime later, and history was made.

The Smirnoff corporation now produces the drink, known these days simply as Mule, as a pre-mixed, ready-to-drink product; it is refreshing enough, but in the cocktail world, the DIY approach is always better.

Generously fill a tall glass with ice cubes, add the ingredients in the order shown, and give the drink a gentle stir. Garnish with a couple of slices of lime.

HARVEY WALLBANGER

A recipe from the 1950s, the Harvey Wallbanger was a beach drink for a constituency that had become sophisticated enough to start mixing obscure liqueurs into their cocktails in Roaring Twenties fashion. It is said, apocryphally, to have been born when a surfing dude named Harvey habitually asked for his vodka-and-orange with a dash of the Italian liqueur Galliano in it. After an unspecified number of these one night, he was seen to walk into a wall in his befuddlement. Like all good cocktail stories, it may or may not be true. One or another bartender at one or another California beach bar formulated the recipe anyway, perhaps as early as 1952.

50 ml/2 ounces plain vodka
freshly squeezed orange juice to
top up
15 ml/½ ounce Galliano

The drink acquired international fame in the 1970s, when it was served on TWA flights. From there, it quickly became a nightclub favourite, and helped boost sales of Galliano, the herb-tinged, bright yellow Tuscan liqueur that comes in a bottle shaped like a classical column.

Pour the vodka and orange into an ice-filled highball glass, and then carefully float the Galliano in a slick on top (pouring over the back of a spoon may help). Garnish with a half-slice of orange.

BLOODY MARY

1 tsp Worcestershire sauce
1 tsp lemon juice
Tabasco to taste
250 ml/9 ounces tomato juice
pinch of celery seasoning
black pepper
50 ml/2 ounces plain vodka

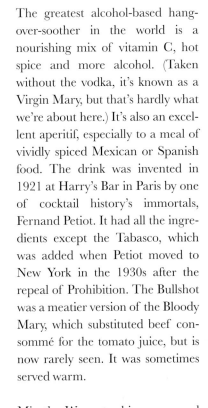

The greatest alcohol-based hang-over-soother in the world is a nourishing mix of vitamin C, hot spice and more alcohol. (Taken without the vodka, it's known as a Virgin Mary, but that's hardly what we're about here.) It's also an excellent aperitif, especially to a meal of vividly spiced Mexican or Spanish food. The drink was invented in 1921 at Harry's Bar in Paris by one of cocktail history's immortals, Fernand Petiot. It had all the ingredients except the Tabasco, which was added when Petiot moved to New York in the 1930s after the repeal of Prohibition. The Bullshot was a meatier version of the Bloody Mary, which substituted beef consommé for the tomato juice, but is now rarely seen. It was sometimes served warm.

Mix the Worcestershire sauce and lemon juice with cracked ice in a tall glass until the ice is nicely seasoned. Add as much Tabasco as you can handle (anything between four drops and a good long shake of the bottle). Top up the glass to an inch or two below the rim with tomato juice, and then add the celery seasoning and two or three twists of the black pepper mill. Add the vodka and give it a good stir. Garnish with a half-slice of lemon and – if you like – a stick of celery, which can be serially dunked in the drink as you eat it.

Endless spins on the Bloody Mary theme have been tried; my own favourite of recent years being the Rising Sun cocktail served in Japanese kaiten bars, in which the Worcestershire is replaced by soy (or shoyu) sauce, the Tabasco with wasabi, and the vodka with sake. In other words, it's not at all the same thing, but it looks similar and is just as good an appetite-whetter.

BLACK RUSSIAN

This was a real reference drink of the 1980s cocktail revival, when one ghastly error in its preparation became the accepted norm. It had been born in the 1950s as a half-and-half mix of vodka and coffee liqueur, archetypally Mexico's Kahlúa. This was a hard, yet luxurious, and very adult mixture, one to be brooded over rather than knocked back unthinkingly. In the eighties, the preferred formula was to substitute the rather sweeter-tasting Tia Maria for the Kahlúa and then drown the whole thing in Coca-Cola. As one who has hated all forms of cola since childhood, I'm biased, but the components do undeniably work for each other.

Stir equal parts plain vodka and coffee liqueur in a tumbler with masses of ice, and don't garnish.

The White Russian is a variation that adds thick cream instead of cola to the basic two ingredients. It is usually shaken with plenty of ice and then strained into a martini glass, but it can also be made as above in a tumbler, and the cream component (in an equal-thirds measure with the alcohol ingredients) floated on top of the drink as though it were a cold Irish Coffee.

If you prefer the naughty cola version, make it in a tall glass and top up to your heart's content. I ain't stopping you.

SEA BREEZE

When cocktails regained their cool in the 1990s, they were often based on earlier recipes that had had some of the sting taken out of them. In many cases, a good slug of vodka was their only alcohol component, in a blend of various fruit juices. The Sea Breeze, now a recognized standard recipe of the International Bartenders' Association, is one such cocktail. It looks and tastes all innocent – a perfect summer quaffer – until you've had a third or fourth.

50 ml/2 ounces plain vodka
75 ml/3 ounces cranberry juice
30 ml/generous 1 ounce yellow grapefruit juice

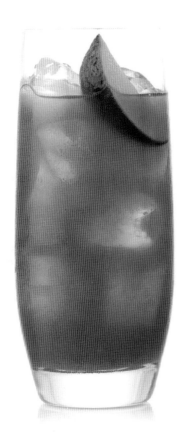

Similar recipes, but with a little more oomph, are the long-established Cosmopolitan (50 ml/ 2 ounces vodka, 20 ml/scant 1 ounce Cointreau, the juice of a lime and 40 ml/1½ ounces cranberry juice, all shaken with ice, strained into a cocktail glass and garnished with a slice of lime), and the 1980s speciality, Woo-Woo (25 ml/ 1 ounce plain vodka, 25 ml/1 ounce peach schnapps and 50 ml/ 2 ounces cranberry juice, poured over ice in a highball glass and garnished with a twist of orange peel).

Pour all the ingredients into a highball glass filled with ice cubes, and garnish with a wedge of lime.

Flavoured vodkas

The modern era has seen a riotous proliferation of flavoured vodkas, the great majority of which are based on fruits, or some combination of fruits. A handful are made with synthetic fruit flavourings, but the most reputable use genuine fruit essences, as well as skins, stones, juice and so forth, in their composition. In singling out eight flavour categories for cocktail recipes in the pages that follow, I have chosen the ones that most naturally (or intriguingly) blend with other flavours in the shapes of liqueurs, fruit juices and other mixers. For the historical background to the development of flavoured vodkas, see the Introduction, pages 34–36.

As well as the flavours selected in the following pages, other good mixers among flavoured vodkas are: **Blackcurrant** and those made with other small berries (which tend to mingle very well with apple juice, as well as good still or sparkling lemonade); **Cherry** (try with white grape juice, ginger beer or lemonade); **Peach** (which makes a sublime mix with orange juice); and **Pear** (perhaps at its best with apple juice, but also good with ginger beer). Try **Chocolate** vodkas in a well-shaken mix with thick cream and plenty of ice for a more grown-up version of the proprietary cream liqueurs, grating a little dark chocolate on to the surface of the drink to finish.

With the variations on **zubrówka**, the traditional bison-grass vodka, the classic mixer is thick, cloudy, pressed apple juice (for more, see Zubrówka, pages 212–213).

Use online resources, too, for ideas. Nearly all the vodka brand websites have sections devoted to mixing their products, with plenty of inspiring cocktail recipes for the newer flavours.

APPLE

Given the traditional role in eastern Europe of apple juice as a blending partner for neutral vodka, apple-flavoured vodkas have been surprisingly slow off the starting blocks. At their best, they have a tangy, crisp aroma and flavour of crunchy green-skinned apple, as well as an appetizing tart character that blends exceptionally well with other flavours. I'm rather partial to the mixture of apple vodka with freshly squeezed orange juice in roughly half-and-half proportions, with a dash of freshly squeezed lime to add zest to the blend.

Smirnoff introduced an impressively aromatic Green Apple flavour in 2008, but my reference product for an apple vodka is Koskenkorva Green Apple from Finland.

Apple Martini

25 ml/1 ounce Koskenkorva Green Apple
50 ml/2 ounces cloudy apple juice
1 tsp grenadine, plus a little extra for dipping

Shake all three ingredients with ice. Dip the rim of a freezer-chilled martini glass into a little more grenadine to get it evenly coated, and then transfer it, still on its rim, to a saucerful of sugar. Don't twist the glass, but lift it cleanly away and you should have a nice pink crystalline rim. Strain the shaken cocktail straight into it, being careful not to let any of the liquid splash the rim. Garnish with a wafer-thin slice of unpeeled red apple. With its twinkling sugar-frosted rim, this would make a fine Christmas cocktail.

COFFEE

I include this because it really is an interesting addition to the repertoire. Until the advent of coffee vodka, Mexico's Kahlúa and Jamaica's Tia Maria were the two principal means of flavouring a cocktail with coffee (short of using coffee itself). The dark brown, svelte flavour of coffee vodka adds an adult note of richness to a blend, and has some surprising mixing abilities, as in the recipe given below.

Stoli Kafya is exotically aromatic and intense, while Van Gogh Double Espresso, a coffee-coloured, mildly sweet concoction, makes a wonderful 50:50 blending partner with Koskenkorva Vanilla, in what feels like a sublime reinvention of the classic Black Russian.

Coffee Apple

Stir equal quantities of Van Gogh Double Espresso and cloudy apple juice (say, 50 ml/2 ounces each) in a mixing jug with ice, then strain into a martini glass. Garnish with a thick slice of sweet-fleshed apple, such as Golden Delicious. This is an unexpectedly delectable combination, although I haven't the faintest idea why it should work as well as it does.

CRANBERRY

Hardly any fruit is more fashionable in cocktail circles these days than cranberry, and the little tart red berries have found their way into many flavoured vodkas, often in conjunction with various other berries such as blueberries, raspberries and blackberries. There is often a slightly more astringent tang to a cranberry vodka than is evident in any of the other berry products, but that makes for a more complex mix. Like raspberry, it blends well with apple juice and a dash of lemon.

Lithuanian Vodka's Cranberry has that interesting, gently bitter character, as does the fine Finlandia Cranberry.

Neapolitan

(adapted from www.drinksmixer.com)

50 ml/2 ounces Finlandia
    Cranberry
15 ml/½ ounce Cointreau
dash of crème de framboise
    (raspberry liqueur) or raspberry
    syrup
dash of Rose's lime cordial

Stir the ingredients with plenty of cracked ice for a minute or two in a mixing jug, then strain into a martini glass. Garnish with a twist of lemon.

As it has virtually no non-alcoholic ingredients, and both of the principal components are a full 40% abv, this is a very grown-up drink, however fun and fruity it tastes.

LEMON

Lemon and other related citrus flavours have been a favoured way of flavouring vodka since the sixteenth century, albeit relying as they did in the frozen north on imported fruit. They live on in the *cytrynówka* and *limonnaya* vodkas of Poland and Russia today, but lemon was also one of the earliest flavours the modern brands tried out once they began to diversify. The tang of lemon (often mingled with lime) is a surefire freshener in a spirit that comes without the added freight of sugar in liqueurs such as limoncello. These vodkas are very crisp and refreshing mixed with orange or cranberry juice, and interestingly dry and acerbic with apple juice, which brings out their citric quality with razor-sharp intensity.

Belvedere Cytrus from Poland, Ireland's Boru Citrus, Grey Goose Le Citron from France and Absolut Citron are all products marked by a strong degree of lemon bite.

Citrus Sunset

25 ml/1 ounce Absolut Citron
25 ml/1 ounce Belvedere
    Pomarańcza
25 ml/1 ounce Rose's lime cordial
soda water to top up

Mix the first three ingredients with plenty of cracked ice in a tall glass, and then top up with soda. Garnish with a wedge of lime and a twist of orange. The combination of orangey Pomarańcza, lemony Citron and lime is a citrus sensation.

LIME

Speaking personally, I find there aren't enough lime vodkas in the world. Of all the citrus fruits, lime makes for the most exotic-tasting of all flavoured vodkas, as unmistakably lively and edgy as it is in the seasoning of Thai cooking. You may find a little goes a long way, but it is a deliciously zesty drink. For mixing, it is perfect with apple juice and a squeeze of lemon, when it helps to deepen and complicate the flavour of the apple very effectively.

Finlandia Lime takes some beating, but Smirnoff has introduced a successful Lime version too.

Outrigger

(from www.drinksmixer.com)

25 ml/1 ounce Finlandia Lime
25 ml/1 ounce peach brandy
25 ml/1 ounce pineapple juice

Shake the ingredients well with ice, then pour into a small tumbler or old-fashioned glass containing plenty of cracked ice. Garnish with a couple of pineapple chunks (fresh is best, but canned will also do, the kind that come in pure juice, not syrup) and a twist of lime.

ORANGE

Vodkas flavoured with one or more members of the orange family make a refreshing change from the plethora of traditional orange-flavoured spirits and liqueurs out there, from Cointreau to Grand Marnier, Mandarine Napoléon to Triple Sec. There is generally a clean, bracing juiciness to the taste, and no syrupy sweetness. They blend especially well with juiced red berries such as raspberry, and also with a range of blended pure fruit juices. One of my more successful experiments was Absolut Mandrin with a British supermarket own-brand juice combining apple, raspberry and white grape.

Absolut Mandrin with its blend of orange and mandarin is a winner, and so are California's Skyy Orange and Grey Goose L'Orange from France.

Mandarin Madness

25 ml/1 ounce Absolut Mandrin
25 ml/1 ounce peach schnapps
15 ml/½ ounce Bols crème de
    banane
dash of grenadine
sparkling lemonade
pineapple juice

Shake the first four ingredients with ice, then strain into a tall glass. Top up with equal parts lemonade and pineapple juice, and garnish with a mandarin segment (from a can will do) and a sliver of strawberry. A riot of exhilarating fruit flavours for a sultry summer evening.

PEPPER

All pepper vodkas are derivatives of the original Polish *pieprzówka* (see page 144), and are seasoned with chilli peppers or peppercorns or both. The degree of spicy hotness can range from a mild smoulder on the palate to the kind of vicious scorching burn that seizes you by the back of the throat. You might think they are impossible to mix with anything, but it ain't necessarily so. They can be quite satisfying with pineapple juice (think of that 1980s' dinner-party favourite, peppered pineapple), when the blend of tropical fruit and hot spice creates a neat counterpoint, but pepper vodka also comes into unlikely balance with pink grapefruit juice and a squeeze of lime, creating a head-spinning assemblage of acerbity and sizzle.

Various versions of *pieprzówka* are made all over Poland, and there are Russian examples too. Absolut Peppar has made all the running in the modern flavoured-vodka era.

Dirty Bloody Martini

25 ml/1 ounce Absolut Peppar
2 tsp dry vermouth
25 ml/1 ounce tomato juice
1 tsp olive brine (from the jar
    of cocktail olives)
twist of black pepper

Shake all the ingredients well with ice to incorporate the tomato juice properly, and then pour out (ice included) into a martini glass. Garnish with a couple of olives – one green, one black. This is a wickedly spicy, dry, savoury drink that makes a highly effective aperitif.

RASPBERRY

Raspberry vodkas at their best offer an altogether charming taste of summer, with the blowsy, juicy-ripe scent of berries picked and nibbled straight off the bush. For simple blending, they are particularly good with cloudy pressed apple juice, livened up with a generous squeeze of lemon. The lemon acts as a seasoning to emphasize the other fruit flavours, and bring the whole mix into focus.

Among notable raspberry vodkas in this book are Absolut Raspberri and Lithuanian Vodka's version, which are both delightful. Blends with cranberry, such as Ireland's Boru Crazzberry and Denmark's Danzka Cranberyraz, are also becoming fashionable. Effen Raspberry and Vanilla, a Dutch vodka, is fabulously creamy in both texture and flavour.

Absolut Raspberri Ambitious

(adapted from www.absolut.com)

50 ml/2 ounces Absolut Raspberri
25 ml/1 ounce cranberry juice
juice of half a lemon
juice of quarter of a lime
sparkling lemonade

Pack a tall glass with ice and add the first four ingredients. Stir, then top up with the lemonade and garnish with a wedge of lemon or lime. This is a fizzier spin on the Cosmopolitan formula (see page 223), and one that will certainly add extra lustre to an afternoon on the beach.

VANILLA

Of all the luxurious flavours in the vodka world, vanilla has become the one most indelibly associated with a senses of adventure and sophistication. It evokes the moment we all discovered real vanilla pods worked such wonders in our desserts, compared with the vanilla essence of a less fortunate age. What is more surprising is that vanilla vodkas are not the greatest mixers. Indeed, I'd say they were the most difficult of flavoured vodkas to find successful blends for. They don't work that well with fruit flavours (although the recipe on this page is an honourable exception), being much better off with chocolate and coffee. Otherwise, neat over ice often seems the best solution.

Stoli Vanil is a widely favoured brand, but I also enjoy Koskenkorva's version from Finland (which has a hint of toffee in it too) and California's Skyy Vanilla, made with Bourbon vanilla beans.

Banana Popsicle

(adapted from www.drinksmixer.com)

25 ml/1 ounce Stoli Vanil
25 ml/1 ounce Bols crème de banane
50 ml/2 ounces orange juice
50 ml/2 ounces pineapple juice

Shake the ingredients with ice, then strain into a small tumbler or old-fashioned glass half-filled with cracked ice. Garnish with a chunk of pineapple and a couple of slices of banana. The next best thing to actually lounging on a Caribbean beach.

Glossary

Alcohol When talking about alcoholic drinks, the word alcohol generally refers to ethanol, or ethyl alcohol. The alcoholic strength of a drink is usually expressed as a percentage of the drink's total volume. It may also be expressed as alcoholic proof (see Proof). Most vodka has between 37.5 and 45% alcohol by volume (abv). In the EU, vodka must have a minimum of 37.5% abv; in the US the minimum for neutral vodkas is 40% abv, while for flavoured vodkas it is 35% abv.

Batch still *see* Pot still

Botanicals Flavourings such as caraway seeds, ginger and lemon peel used in drinks; they are usually strained or filtered out, so only their flavour remains in the finished product.

Column still *see* Continuous still

Condenser The part of the still that turns the vapour (alcohol) back into liquid.

Congeners Natural compounds that give aroma and flavour to alcoholic drinks.

Continuous still Also known as a column still or patent still. In this process, the distillation occurs as one uninterrupted process, with the unwanted portions of the distillate continuously removed while the procedure is under way. This procedure is used now for the vast majority of vodkas, and for France's armagnac. The older alternative (*see* Pot still) is to reload the distillate into the still for subsequent distillations.

Distillation The process in which alcohol is extracted from fermented liquids.

Ethanol, ethyl alcohol The chemical name for alcohol.

Fermentation The conversion, by yeasts, of sugars (present in grains, potatoes or other ingredients) into alcohol and carbon dioxide.

Genetic modification or manipulation (GM) Biotechnology can change the genes of plants in order to make them resistant to disease, drought, etc. It has been practised for more than 30 years, but its long-term effects on human health, local ecosystems and the global environment are still a matter of dispute. Organic produce is never genetically modified.

Mash The mixture of heated water and crushed grain (or other ingredients) that will ferment and produce an alcoholic liquid; the liquid can then be distilled to produce spirits.

Methanol The toxic form of alcohol, it has a lower boiling point than other forms of alcohol and is thus the first to be vaporized during distillation. Distillers remove this part of the distilled liquid.

Organic Organic foods and drinks are produced without the use of synthetic fertilizers and pesticides; produce may not be genetically modified.

Pot still Also known as a batch still, this is the traditional method of distillation. The fermented liquid is heated by direct heat; the vapours are collected and led off into the condenser, where they are cooled by running water and reliquefy as spirit. The spirit will go through at least two distillations, so this is known as a batch process. It is used for some artisanal vodkas, as well as for cognac. It is a less efficient process than continuous distillation (see Continuous still opposite).

Proof Until 1980, spirits sold in the UK were labelled with degrees proof rather than with a percentage of alcohol by volume (abv). 100° proof was the equivalent of 57.15% abv and was the most dilute spirit that would allow gunpowder to ignite. Sailors tested or 'proofed' their rum ration by dousing it in gunpowder; if the gunpowder did not catch fire, the rum was too weak ('under proof') and had probably been watered down. In the United States, labels must state the percentage of alcohol by volume; they may also state proof, which in the US is defined as twice the percentage of alcohol by volume, so 40% abv = 80 proof.

Rectification Part of the process of continuous distillation, in which some of the distilled, alcohol-rich liquid is fed back from the condenser on to a series of plates where the rising vapour is passing. They interact so that some of the vapour liquefies, and some of the distilled liquid vaporizes, in effect creating a redistillation.

Addresses

Index of flavoured vodkas

Index

Acknowledgments

The author and publishers would like to thank all the vodka suppliers for their help with sourcing vodkas for the tastings and photography; also the Gin & Vodka Association of Great Britain, Daisy Jones at the *Spirits Business* magazine, Saverglass for the bottle for the front jacket image, Nicki Dowey for the cocktail photography, Michael Wicks for the bottle photography and Barking Dog Art for the map on page 23.

Picture acknowledgments
Absolut page 37; Anova Books/Savoy Cocktail Book page 21; Agripic pages 2, 27 (below left); Alamy/Mary Evans Picture Library page 29; Bridgeman Art Library pages 10, 14, 169; Corbis pages 20, 25, 27 (above left and below right); Diageo/Smirnoff page 170; Nicki Dowey pages 42–45, 214–215, 217, 218, 219, 220, 221, 222, 223, 225, 226, 227, 228, 229, 230, 231, 232, 233; Getty Images/Hulton Archive/Fred Mayer page 32; Philip Hollis page 35; David King pages 16, 19; Kobal Collection page 22; Photolibrary page 38; Shutterstock pages 8–9; Svensk Vodka page 28; Visualrian/Novosti page 27 (above right).